THE DEBRIEF IMPERATIVE

Fighter Pilots and The Secret Tool That Is Transforming Businesses
The World over

James D. Murphy and William M. Duke

Published by FastPencil, Inc.

"Every manager understands that organizational learning is critical for success in today's volatile markets. But few know how to squeeze insight and improvement out of experience. The Debrief Imperative offers concrete guidance on how individuals, teams, and organizations can learn from their mistakes."
- Donald Sull, Professor of Management Practice, London Business School

To my colleagues at Afterburner Inc:
This book is a culmination of 16 years of great ideas you have cultivated and tested in our Flawless Execution Model. You, our clients, and our friends make it better every day. This book and our increasingly more effective intellectual property are the result of our maniacal dedication to our debriefing process at Afterburner. I want to especially thank my writing partner Will Duke and Brigadier General Charles Campbell USAF (ret.) for their specific oversight, insight, and passion for what we do.
Murph

⚳

CONTENTS

FOREWORD: The Secret Weapon of Success

Not long after graduating from college, I joined an office products company and started selling copiers. I loved what I did. I made good money, trusted the products I sold, loved my customers and quickly rose to the top, until I was the #1 sales rep for the entire company. But something was missing. I wasn't dissatisfied but I could feel something was not entirely right about my life. One Saturday afternoon a friend of mine talked me into going down to his Air National Guard base to see what was going on. We got out on the ramp, walked out to his jet, and he had me climb up into the cockpit. It was transforming; I felt it in an instant. This was meant for me, this cockpit. *This* was what I was missing.

Now, nothing in my ancestral tree pointed in this direction; in fact, no one in my family had ever served in the military, but sitting in the cockpit of that fighter jet was a turning point in my life. I knew then that I was going to walk away from a successful sales career and become a fighter pilot. I had no flight experience, I loved the job I had, but I was going to fly jets.

Thankfully, the Air Force saw fit to let me join their ranks. Just two years after signing up I was not only flying, I was flying the supersonic F-15 Eagle, unquestionably the most sophisticated and admired jet in the sky. I was soon to become a flight lead in my unit and an instructor pilot. How could that have happened?

The truth is, I unwittingly stepped into a battle-honed system designed to squeeze every ounce of performance out of a flight candidate, designed to sharpen their skills to a level of perfection few attain —so much so that it was utterly natural for the Air Force to turn over a $30 million jet to me, a freshly minted pilot whose only previous experience was selling copiers. And guess what? They had total confidence in me after just 24 months of training.

I flew missions all over the world. I trained on new weapons systems and learned new tactics and practiced daily on combat maneuvers and emergency procedures. I flamed out an engine at night in a storm over the Pacific Ocean, nursed it back to life and got home safely. I had skills and instincts I never knew existed and I was performing at a level I had never experienced before. I felt unbeatable.

One night I realized that if I had been trained like this in the copier business, I would have been unstoppable. If I had known then what I knew now, if I had had the insights, the way of thinking, the patterns —I mean, it was clear to me that the exact same processes that turned me into a fighter pilot in less than 24 months could be a textbook for turning the average Joe into a flawlessly executing, turning-and-burning businessman or businesswoman. So I started making notes on the discipline, the practices, our planning.

Then I started a company. Today, Afterburner Inc. has trained more than 1.5 million business leaders in the very same techniques that turned me, and tens of thousands of people like me, into the world's finest fighter pilots. Since we opened our doors in 1996, we've been to 23 countres all over the world teaching a method we now call Flawless Execution. Chances are, if you work for a Fortune 500 company, you know us. Chances are, if you know us, you know that the most important part of Flawless Execution is the debrief.

If you know that much, then you know this: debriefing is an art that flows priceless information back into a company; debriefing lies at the heart of what keeps fighter pilots alive and superior in the air; debriefing is what keeps companies alive and ahead of their competition. Debriefing is all about continuous improvement. Think about that —continuous improvement. Getting better every day. Being better at your job every day. Recording those precious victories we all need to excel every day.

Debriefing is a specialized technique refined over millions of hours of flying and decades of trial and error in military aviation. As you will read, it was developed by both the U.S. Navy and Air Force and is used after every military flight, bar none. It has saved countless lives, led to near-instantaneous improvements in systems, practices, and plans, and is making the next generation of pilots better than the last. It's also the secret tool that's transforming businesses, from consumer package goods to restaurant chains to financial institutions. For 16 years we've been training companies in the art of the debrief. For 16 years we've been refining that tool into the book you have now.

Before you think this book is going to take you back to the school-house and ruin your day, think about your own life. As fighter pilots, we debriefed *every* mission we flew. For instance, after a simulated air-to-air combat mission, we'd come home, take off our name tags, peel off our rank, get into a room and talk it over. Nothing held back. *How'd we do? Where did we go wrong? What did the adversaries throw at us that we hadn't planned for? Were the plans clear?* The debrief helped us perform better as a group and perform better as individuals. It was all about us —and what's more fun than talking about what you love to do?

Now, relate this to yourself. At some point in your life you were probably pretty good at debriefing, though you may not have known it. For most of us, that time occured when we were playing a team sport like football, soccer, or basketball. Remember how you'd huddle up to figure out what was going right or going wrong? Remember the chalk talks with the coaches to map out the second half, based on the results of the first half? That's continuous improvement. That's debriefing. You broke it down, found the root causes, drew up some new plays and went back out on the field.

When you think about it, you've been doing something like this, *at some level,* all your life; we teach how to do it at a high level for the *rest* of your life. When you finish this book you'll be better at whatever you do, no exceptions. In fact, have the whole team read this and watch what happens. Things will start to click. Your group will come together in ways you never thought possible. You'll be making fewer mistakes. You'll be innovating. You'll be breaking down stubborn problems and finding the root causes and fixing things once and for all. And If you own the company, your company will break away from the competition and start to become the leader, a profitable leader.

Every one of the nearly 50 people who work for our company knows the power of our Stealth Debrief process. And if we ever take it for granted, our clients are the first to tell us what it's done for them. *Debriefing made us a better company. Debriefing pumped millions of dollars of good ideas back into our company. Stealth got us to the root cause of a problem that's been bugging us forever and fixed it once and for all. Debriefing made us more effective, more profitable, more powerful. The Stealth Debrief gave our people a sense of belonging.* And it didn't matter if they were in the financial sector, hospitality, manufacturing, packaged goods or health care; the debrief was transforming.

The simple act of assessing what went right or wrong at the end of any task, project, or mission is a learning opportunity that simply can't be ignored. The Stealth Debrief is intended to help you close the learning gap, to flow information back into the company, to fix things once and for all, and to accelerate the learning experiences for everyone until, ever so imperceptibly, you start to pull away from the competition — then one day you discover you're #1.

The Stealth Debrief. That's our secret weapon —as fighter pilots and as business leaders —to accelerate performance and win.

Happy Hunting!

James D. "Murph" Murphy
Afterburner, Inc., January 2011

A CULTURE OF PLANNING

ONE OF OUR CLIENTS had an expression that really resonated with me. He was the head of training in a large restaurant chain. He said that they were good at managing in the gray areas, the places where there aren't hard-and-fast rules. I liked that expression, managing in the gray areas. It seemed so truthful, that we have gray areas; I know your company does. But how do you become proficient at managing the unknown? I asked him. He said it was alignment—that everyone in their restaurants knew what the overall company goals were, that they had standards for just about every contingency and they debriefed their experiences with regularity.

We all need a goal. We all need to know where we're headed. If we don't know where we're headed we can't develop a plan that gets us there. The fact is, not only do we need a goal; more importantly, we need a goal that's articulated in minute detail. The more detail we use to express our vision, our goal, the more certain we can be that the entire organization knows where we're headed and how we want to get there—and the more certain we can be that the entire organization is aligned around it, the more certain we can be that we've empowered our people to take control, to execute their part of the plan, to do the right things in the gray areas.

So, what does it mean to break down a vision into the tiniest detail? One of my favorite examples is the company picnic. In my mind, a company picnic is hot dogs, tubs of beer, colas and chips and a company softball game. In your mind, a company picnic could be a red-and-white tablecloth and a basket of wine and cheese, or a river cruise catered by a Cajun chef with a jazz band playing in the background. It's no good for either of us to ask someone to plan a company picnic unless we give them our vision, unless we tell them exactly what we mean. Once they know I want hot dogs and softball, they'll figure out the mustard, pickle relish and buns. After the picnic is over, we can measure our actions against my goal. Did we serve hot dogs? Yep. Did we have a softball game? Yep.

Overly simplified for sure, but that's what I mean by expressing a goal in detail. Everyone executing the plan for the company picnic was aligned and they knew what I wanted. Their actions achieved my vision down to mustard and relish. Okay, that's basic business and we'll get back to it in a moment, but the takeaway here is that people execute their daily missions against a plan based on a clear picture of the expected outcome.

Now let's look at it from the other side of the fence. What if you don't have a plan? What if your people don't have a clue to your vision or how that breaks down into the plans that they are supposed to execute? Let's pretend for a moment; let's say you're in the business of planning and staging high-end company events and I call you to do my hot-dogs-and-softball company outing. I explain what I want and how many people we'll have and I give you the job of pulling it off. Unfortunately, when I get there it's not quite right. Yes, there are baseballs and softballs and we have a field to play on, but the hot dogs are bratwursts. Now, I don't like bratwurst; I love hot dogs and hot dogs are hot dogs, not brats. Nathan's didn't make Nathan's Famous brats, they made Nathan's Famous hot dogs. Hot dogs are synonymous with Coney Island. Hot dogs and baseball and ballparks. I wanted hot dogs, not bratwurst.

What went wrong? Clearly it wasn't us. When we debriefed the picnic, my manager showed me the order form he received from the event planners and it clearly said hot dogs. I called the president of the event planning company and was referred to a junior associate who told me that I should be grateful that their meat buyer was able to upgrade us to brats at no extra cost. But that's not what I wanted.

What do you suppose happened inside that company? Let's guess. Let's say the company's basic business model was to handle 50 events a week, charge through the roof, save money by extracting deals from the vendor, incentivize employees based on the profits each event generates, and move on to the next 50 events. That's a pretty typical business model, I have no problem with that. To run fifty events, they must have 5 site planners, 12 food buyers, 20 trucks, and 60 venue managers who handle set-ups and breakdowns. In the end, they would have no idea who ordered the food for my particular picnic or why I was unhappy. They had upgraded me to brats, after all.

But that's not what I wanted, and worse, my complaint went nowhere. But then it happened again. Someone got brats instead of hot dogs or a three-tiered wedding cake instead of a two-tiered wedding cake—little mistakes, time and time again. Can you see how the small things can undermine an entire company? Even when you think you're doing it right, you could be doing it wrong; if you don't have a process for uncovering those little mistakes *even when you think you're doing it right*, you could be doing it wrong. Clear goals stated in minute detail require a system to evaluate the execution of that plan after all is said and done. How did we do? *Not so hot, the client complained.* Why? *They wanted hot dogs and got brats.* Why did that happen? *Our meat buyer was offered a special so he upgraded them to brats.* Who said that was an upgrade? *Well, it is.* But that's not what the client ordered. *Yes, but that's how we make our bonuses here—profit per event.*

Here's the point. As businessmen and women we come from a culture of planning. Business school teaches you to write plans. Venture capitalists want to see your plan. The sales department has a sales plan. The finance department has a plan. Plans for this and plans for that. Good plan or bad, you have to have a plan.

That's good, but it's not enough. Where business remains exceptionally weak is in the area of self-analysis. We're not very good at holding ourselves up to the plan and analyzing how well we did. We're not very good at examining the results of a plan, the effectiveness of a plan, or how our people executed their part of plan; and that's a terrible opportunity loss. Plans are like a pair of bookends: they don't work without the other half, the debrief.

The Stealth Debrief starts with a clear picture of the mission, the plan, then uses a battle-tested format to measure ourselves against the desired outcome, against the plan. It's ying and yang. If my vision is for hot dogs and softball, then we can measure ourselves against the actual outcome. If my vision is a river cruise with Cajun food and a jazz band, then we can measure ourselves. And if my company produces events, our teams can measure themselves against their plans, such as how well they staged a hot-dogs-and-softball event for my company.

Plans and debriefing; debriefing and plans. We state the plan, we communicate it to the participants, then we can engage the incredible power of the debrief. Any variation to the stated plan is easy to identify. Brats for hot dogs? *Nope, not what the client wanted.* Why did that happen? *We have a system that incentivizes the wrong behavior.* Corrections are instantaneous. Improvement occurs overnight. We transform ourselves. Plans and debriefs; debriefs and plans. We debrief *all* the time, and we do it for one overriding reason: to improve. To identify what worked and what didn't; to find root causes of problems and to feed those solutions back into the company *that day*. We call this continuous improvement.

Continuous Improvement

> *"A learning culture must therefore value reflection and experimentation, and must give its members the time and resources to do it."*
>
> –Edgar H. Schein
> Organizational Culture and Leadership, 3rd Ed.

If there was one trend in the last decade of the twentieth century that anyone would recognize as important, it would be *continuous improvement*. Whether it was branded the Deming Method or Six Sigma or a host of other models, "continuous improvement processes" found their way into organizations large and small and have made a major contribution to improving quality worldwide.

In an environment of instant and unpredictable change, most of these models are statistically based and unwieldy. They can bog down a company and delay actions and reactions so much that they become ends instead of means. To survive, thrive, and remain on the cutting edge, organizations must learn to adapt rapidly, which means they need feedback loops that are nearly instantaneous and a process for feeding lessons learned back into the company in near-real time. They must close the gap between what was true about the market yesterday and what the new truth is today.

The new paradigm: Time is your enemy.

The new paradigm: Speed is everything.

The new paradigm: Lessons learned are essential to your competitive advantage. We embrace a culture of continuous improvement, we embrace a culture of learning.

A Culture of Learning

When you think about it, aviation is by necessity a culture of learning. In one flight alone we can go through three time zones, four weather fronts, and make a dozen changes in altitudes or headings. We may take off in Greenland and land in the heat and humidity of Panama. We train and retrain on the aircraft systems, the regulations, the standards, the normal procedures and the emergency procedures. It's our job to get the plane down safely, whether riddled by bullets or with two dead engines snuffed out by birds over the Hudson River.

So we aviators seek cultures of learning. Cultures of learning are marked by questions such as "Can I get your opinion on this?" and "What do you think about that?" and "How did you handle the problem?" In a culture of learning, we don't believe it's a sign of weakness to make a mistake; we think it's a weakness to hide our mistakes. That's what we mean by a culture of learning. In that type of culture, continuous improvement is just that—continuous.

I just flew through a patch of bumpy air. I feed that back into the in-flight advisory system, which passes it on to other pilots, who augment my real-time experience with hard radar data. That's a symptom of a culture of learning. If we flew a four-ship F-15 mission, we get into one room and take apart every phase of the mission as soon as we land. If we did everything as briefed, terrific. But if we saw a new enemy tactic, we feed that data back into the squadron so the next guys are ready for it. If we burned through too much gas, we dig down to find out why. Did we spend too much time in afterburner? Were the refueling tankers where they were supposed to be? Was the weather briefing wrong and we had a headwind when we expected a tailwind?

We don't hide our weaknesses.
Rather, we think it weak to hide our mistakes.

Stealth Debrief

The Stealth Debrief is a simple process performed in discrete blocks of time. You insert debriefing into the day-to-day execution of your business plan, as one of four components of an organizational and continuous improvement methodology called *Flawless Execution*. Flawless Execution is a cyclical process divided into four parts: plan, brief, execute and debrief. Each of these four components are interconnected and interrelated, forming a whole that is greater than the sum of its parts.

The planning component focuses on team collaboration to create better plans through an iterative process of rapid improvement. Within the planning process is a step that includes the incorporation of lessons learned. These lessons learned are the quantifiable product of the debrief process. It is the lesson learned that formally completes the Flawless Execution cycle.

Again, businesses have a culture of planning; the gap between plans and a highly effective, continuously improving, flawlessly executing company is filled by the debrief.

In the 1950s and 1960s, during the build-up and at the height of the Cold War, It was absolutely true to say that the United States Air Force's nuclear Strategic Air Command had a simple formula for grading pilot proficiency. If you received a 100, you passed. If you received a 99, you failed. Thirty years later, I experienced similar criteria in my fighter pilot career, when a pilot was given only two flights to correct a deficiency or it was all over. The same was true of the Navy fighter pilots. There are no points for second place.

> *"In today's penny-pinched environment, you can't afford to send employees to events without capturing what they learn. The model? The military debriefing. You need a systematic approach to what was once an informal process, a practice woven into the fabric of organizational life."*
>
> –Jimmy Guterman
> "The Lost Art of Debriefing," Harvard Business Review, March 2002.

But that was not always the case.

As pilots, our DNA goes back to those romantic barnstormers that flew dangerously close to a crowd, broke all of the rules, wowed the audiences, and sported a razor-thin Rhett Butler mustache. Flying was a seat-of-the-pants business. Turn-and-burn, yank-and-bank; show me how to start the engine and get out of my way.

But then we sobered up. We were forced to change. There were too many accidents, too many crashes, too many fatalities. The training intensified and basic skills such as instrument flying and navigation replaced the prerequisites of dash-and-charm as a pilot credential.

Still, we had a long way to go. During World War II, the success of a mission was measured by how many people got back alive, and the debrief was largely the battle damage report. Crews were interviewed by the intelligence officers to identify new anti-aircraft emplacements or new enemy tactics, but little heed was paid to the execution of the mission, how tight the formations were flown, if the navigational way-points were correct or if the proper landing procedures were used to penetrate thick ground fog during an instrument landing. Bone-weary pilots simply hungered for sleep and that was that.

It wasn't until Vietnam that we started to take debriefing seriously, and that came about only because we were suffering terrible casualities in the sky. During the early part of the war we were losing one aircraft to every 3.7 enemy aircraft shot down, and at some points it was as low as 2:1. At first that might sound like a successful statistic, but in truth it was abysmal. Considering the training our pilots had and the superior jets they were flying, the kill ratio should have been much higher.

But it wasn't. The problem was the first 10 missions. We quickly discovered that on-the-job training in real combat has tragic results. Our pilots were so overwhelmed, so Task Saturated by real combat that by the time they got up to speed, half of their buddies were gone. We had to accelerate their learning curve, get them combat-wise fast, get pilots battle hardened before they flew their first combat mission. Tall order.

We went back to the basics. If our pilots were too green going into combat, then our training had to change until they were too good to be shot down during their entire tour of duty. The answer was to marry an academic approach to an intense, near-combat flight training regime followed by a rigorous analysis of the results. We were going to train our pilots to fly hard. We were going to force them to make mistakes. And then we were going to help them understand their mistakes. We were going to create a culture where there was no place to hide, where mistakes led to winning, where everything would be analyzed, a place where there were no points for second best, a place these pilots could train until they were better than their instructors. The Air Force created the Fighter Weapons School, followed many years later by the Navy's famous Top Gun school.

It was in these schools, born of necessity, that the debrief entered military aviation as a deadly serious tool of executional excellence. A group of pilots would be given a plan for a sortie; they'd fly it, then they'd get in a room and analyze it, and that was where the breakthroughs came. The post-flight analysis was as hard and as unforgiving and as brutally honest as it could be. First, the mission leader would restate the mission objectives and the results. Did we accomplish our mission objective? If yes, how? If no, how? Every detail of the mission would be analyzed, from the briefing, start, taxi, takeoff, route and the tactical mission, to the return to base, landing and taxi in. And we wanted to know *why* things occurred. Why did you stack high in the formation with the sun high on the horizon? Why did you perform a reversal instead of a ditch maneuver? Why did the #3 aircraft in our four-ship come back with 1,000 pounds less fuel than the others?

We wired the training areas and gathered telemetry so we could recreate the engagements on big screens. No one could hide; mistakes were bigger than life. We broke every minute of a mission down to its fundamental parts, until we had pilots who were deadly serious about flying and surviving.

From there, it spread. Pilots went back to their units and instituted debriefs. Missions never ended at the bar, they ended in the debriefing room. The debrief became a place where everyone could hash it out in detail, what went right, what went wrong, and what could be done about it next. It became open and honest, nameless and rankless. It was refined, tweaked and improved until *how* a debrief was run was as important as *what* the debrief covered.

Pilots got a lot better. Executional excellence became the accepted norm rather than the exception. The debrief led to continuous improvement and accelerated learning across entire squadrons and entire wings. We learned to apply strict time limits and to manage the process so information moved into the debrief quickly. (Nothing worse than endless meetings with pointless conversations.) In the end, our pilots started to survive their first 10 missions and the kill ratios improved sixfold, from 2:1 to 13:1.

The debriefs that fighter pilots now hold are places where participants freely admit their mistakes and make absolutely sure they understand their successes. They develop lessons learned, lessons that can immediately improve existing processes and can be stored and transmitted to any other pilot, anywhere in the world, to improve their planning and execution. Debriefs dig deeply into root causes, where powerful organizational improvements can be made.

What About Your Company?

We've trained hundreds of thousands of executives in the Stealth Debrief. We've seen it transform companies big and small. People who begin using debriefing want more of it, and it spreads across departments and into the core company processes, such as the manufacturing process or the distribution arm.

You may think you're too small or too hierarchal for the Stealth Debrief; it may sound like a tall order for your company. But consider this—formal debriefing takes place in the most hierarchical institution of all, the military, where rank is quite literally worn on everyone's shoulder or sleeve. If the military can do it, any organization can.

We know. Because we train them.

CONTINUOUS IMPROVEMENT

INSPIRED BY THE ZERO-TOLERANCE-FOR-ERROR world of combat aviation, Flawless Execution is a framework for success in any rapidly changing business environment. Within that framework is the specific form of debriefing we've been talking about called the Stealth Debrief, something we'll explain by breaking it down to the letters in the word: S.T.E.A.L.T.H. But before we get to S.T.E.A.L.T.H., lets unpack the Flawless Execution Model and understand where we are today.

Flawless

In a word, *flawless* means perfect. Arguably, there is no such thing. Flawless Execution is not about perfection. Instead, it is about the *endless pursuit of flawless execution*. It is an obsession with failure, both as something to be avoided *and* as something to be respected for the learning it provides. In our complex world, there can never be any guarantees of success. But mistakes and errors provide us with invaluable experiences about ourselves, our organizations, and our world. Mistakes and errors enable us to be more successful in the future and adapt to changing circumstances, if we learn from them. As I said earlier, we don't see mistakes as a weakness; we think hiding mistakes is the ultimate weakness. *Flawless* is an unattainable goal that propels us to ever greater performance and success.

Execution

Execution means getting things done. But, what things? Well, the right things, of course. What are the right things? The right things are those things we *plan* to do. Today's business culture is a culture of planning and plans. From its inception, every organization began with a plan. A company grows and succeeds as the result of planning. How do we measure our plans? As I've said, the step so often overlooked in business is the debrief, the after-action report that puts the plan, and the people executing the plan, under the cold light of real results.

So, what is Flawless Execution? Flawless Execution is a holistic system of simple, interdependent processes that enables individuals, teams, and organizations to accelerate their performance in the rapidly changing, challenging, and complex world.

In effect, it is a meta-process—a process for managing and mastering the change that the complexity of our modern world creates. At its core, it is a simple means by which the individuals within an organization can more effectively improve to achieve their goals.

Flawless Execution is a model designed to assist organizations in developing a high-performing culture. To understand how Flawless Execution enables that development, one needs to understand some terms utilized throughout this book: *system*, *organization*, and *continuous improvement*.

System

A *system* can be described as a complex, interdependent process.[1] A human being is a system. A company is a system; so is a government or an economy. The global economy is a system of systems, a *supersystem* that continually changes in unpredictable ways. Systems are typically interdependent with other larger and smaller systems. What one system does affects other systems which, in turn, affects the originating system in a continuously complex interaction.

Systems are incredibly complex; think of human anatomy. Complex systems, because they are interdependent, affect each other in a variety of unpredictable ways. As an example, the human system—me —gets into the automotive system—my BMW— with potentially millions of outcomes. Therefore, nothing is truly predictable and everything has some potential for failure. It is precisely these variables, the complex behavior of systems, that cause the rapid change and unpredictability prevalent in our modern world.

Within this unpredictable world of complex systems, organizations struggle to manage predictable processes, the manufacturing process, the sales process, the distribution process, the innovation process, etc., at a controlled level of quality. But if everything is part of a complex system that is unpredictable, how is it that we can speak of predictable processes existing within unpredictable systems? That is why organizations must *organize*.

Organization

Organization is a broad term that originates from living systems. Its root, *organ*, implies coordination and cooperation among other living things. Thus, an organization is a group of people working together. In Flawless Execution, the term organization is used in two slightly different senses. First, it is used as a blanket designation for any business or company, government entity, association, and so forth. In that sense an organization is an association of individuals created for some coordinated purpose. Second, organization is used more specifically to describe the degree to which those individuals coordinate well. In this sense, organization applies to the quality and value of the processes utilized within an organization.

Organizations organize in many ways. They organize from the physical means of laying out office space and conference rooms to the organization of information management. The most effective means of being organized is through processes. Processes provide a "script" for our daily activities. They tell us what has worked in the past so we don't have to recreate the wheel every day.

Processes simply take specific input and produce specific output via a set of predetermined tasks. Processes are developed within organizations to solve problems and meet challenges more effectively and efficiently. I need a process for making my products, so I create a manufacturing process. I need to sell my products so I create a selling process.

But processes also tend to get institutionalized; they tend to become rigid and start to resist change. "We've done it this way for ten years," is a common symptom of that resistance. In our fighter pilot world it was the most experienced and often the best pilots who had the hardest time adapting to change.

But processes must change—they *have* to change—if we are to adapt, stay current, or get ahead. Changing or evolving processes over time is one of the most popular and powerful concepts in management today. We've said it before; we call this *continuous improvement*. Let's break that down.

Continuous Improvement

Continuous improvement is a commonly used phrase that refers to the improvement of processes. It does not refer to the improvement of organizations in a holistic way because organizations are complex systems. Systems either survive, thrive, and achieve a high level of performance or they stagnate, decline, and die—survival of the fittest writ large. Therefore, organizations themselves do not continuously improve per se, but rather their internal processes continuously improve. The sum of what could be improvements in hundreds, if not thousands of processes within an organization, when taken together, evolves the system called the company, and allows the company to make an exponential leap forward.

If my marketing department's new product development process is 100% efficient and my manufacturing is 100% efficient and my creative platforms for my social media strategies are executed perfectly, the effect on the system called my company could be a 500% increase in market value, a tremendous increment over the sum of the parts. (Just look at the iPod and the iPhone to see the impact they've had on Apple's market cap). The trick is creating an organization that embraces change in their processes, adopts the best of the changes and lets these changes flow into the marketplace. These organizations develop a culture of learning and embrace continuous improvement because they do their best *not* to resist change. They're fighter pilots, leaning forward, trying to improve continuously.

The purpose of Flawless Execution is to aid organizations in both continuously improving processes and providing an organized approach to continuously adapting to the complex challenges and unpredictable changes inherent in the modern world.

Let's bring this full circle. Businesses have created a culture of planning, but execution takes place within complex systems that are the sum of processes that must continuously adapt to change, lest a company stagnate and die. Flawless Execution is a holistic system of simple, interdependent processes that enables individuals, teams, and organizations to accelerate their performance in the rapidly changing, challenging, and complex world through a circular processes called plan-brief-execute-debrief. Properly implemented, Flawless Execution is a model designed to assist organizations in developing a high-performing culture. High performing cultures never hide their weaknesses; rather, they embrace a culture of learning and use the Stealth Debrief to trigger continuous improvement.

Now let's unpack Flawless Execution once and for all so we can set up the Stealth Debrief. Flawless Execution is structured in a pyramid of seven tiers with the Flawless Execution Cycle occupying the central and most significant of the seven tiers. The tiers are, from top to bottom:

Future Picture

An organization's Future Picture is a clear, compelling, high-resolution description of the future that the organization desires to realize.[2] It is not just a description of the organization, but a description of the organization and its surrounding system. A Future Picture answers two questions: What will this organization look like? and How will it change the market, community, or even the world?

The Future Picture development process begins by assembling a diverse team to collaboratively build and improve situational awareness, or the "big picture" internal and external to their organization. Once they have a clear understanding of all the myriad forces at work inside and outside the organization, the planning team develops the high-resolution detail that makes up the Future Picture through a series of clear statements that may include descriptions in some or all of the following areas: financial and market position, business areas, innovation, insider and outsider perception, workforce characteristics, brand, corporate culture and citizenship, ownership, and incentive philosophy. And, since a lack of objective measurements means there can be no clear determination of success, measurements are essential components of each of these statements.

Together, the collection of statements from these areas create the high-resolution picture of the future that serves as a compelling objective and forms the basis of planning, decision making, revision and adaptation for the entire organization. As management gurus Noel Tichy and Warren Bennis have noted, a vision (Future Picture) should be a "storyline" that is both solid enough to stand the test of time and flexible enough to adapt to changing circumstances in order for leaders at all levels to develop subplots and stories.[3] Because Flawless Execution is *fractal* (composed of self-similar parts), it allows for and encourages the development of such successive subplots and stories in the form of a series of supporting strategic and tactical plans. These cascading plans align the organization from top to bottom in the pursuit of the overarching Future Picture.

Strategy

The Flawless Execution approach to developing strategy focuses upon systems (network) analysis and theory. Because complex systems are in a constant state of change yet tend to resist efforts to control that change, an effective strategy must address their natural structure. Complex systems tend to organize themselves into a network of nodes. Within those systems, a few large nodes will hold significant influence over the others. It is those primary nodes, or *centers of gravity*, that should be the focal points of an organization's strategic plans.[4] In Flawless Execution, the organization maps out the various internal and external systems, identifies the centers of gravity (or COGs), and develops clear, measurable, and achievable plans. These plans express how the organization will affect each COG through a statement of desired effect with specific measurements. Together, this collection of plans forms the overall strategic plan to achieve the Future Picture.

Leader's Intent

Plans should not be handed down from the ivory tower, the senior leadership in an organization. Instead, effective planning must be a process that cascades downward through the organization. Planning must also be open or collaborative, that is, open to several layers of leadership and specialists, and should include the team that will execute the plan. For these reasons, the leader's intent is a *statement of desired effect*. Leaders need to communicate what they intend for others to accomplish rather than tell them what to do.

The Flawless Execution Cycle

The four-part Flawless Execution Cycle is a simple yet powerful methodology. It is a cyclical, interdependent model used at every level of planning and execution, from the Future Picture to the strategy and on down to the day-to-day planning and execution on the organization's front line.

The Execution Cycle is organized into four basic processes and their corresponding techniques: plan, brief, execute, and debrief.

Plan: Flawless Execution utilizes a six-step planning model.

1. State the Mission Objective
2. Identify Threats
3. Identify Resources
4. Evaluate Lessons Learned
5. Develop a Course of Action with individual accountability
6. Plan for Contingencies

Brief: Flawless Execution utilizes a formal brief, a disciplined form of communication that prepares the team to execute more effectively.

1. Brief the Scenario
2. Restate the Mission Objective
3. Identify the Top Threats and Resources
4. Execution – the Final Plan
5. Flexibility – Contingencies

Execute: Flawless Execution provides a collection of techniques to improve execution and manage *Task Saturation,* the perception or reality of having too much to do and too little time or resources to do it.

1. Six Fundamental Keys to Successful Execution – *L.O.C.K.E.D. on Teams* model
2. Mutual Support – the 'Wingman' concept
3. Checklists
4. Crosschecks and Task Shedding

Debrief: One of the most powerful tools in the Flawless Execution Cycle is the continuous improvement and learning achieved through proper debriefing. The Stealth Debrief model, the subject of this book, is essential to basic process continuous improvement; it accelerates experience and learning and develops a culture of learning in organizations.

1. Set the Time
2. Tone – Nameless and Rankless
3. Execution vs. Objectives
4. Analyze Execution
5. Lessons Learned – Develop Actionable Lessons
6. Transfer Lessons Learned – Save and Transmit throughout the organization
7. High Note – Recap Results in a positive manner

Standards

Standards provide the basic guidance, or doctrine, within an organization that guides execution. Standards may describe the proper use of processes or behaviors, but they are not processes in themselves. The objective of standards is to provide guidance when dealing with complex challenges. Standards only provide the minimum guidance for individuals and teams, in order for them to execute effectively.

Training

Training aligns with the Future Picture, the strategy or the subordinate plans necessary to execute the strategy and achieve the Future Picture. Training that does not necessarily or directly support these plans or the carrying out of daily operations or processes may broadly be categorized as *education*, important but not essential. Training must first define what must be learned; then the learning must be demonstrated by effective trainers. Finally, the learner must perform the learning. Training that does not assess the learners' proficiency cannot be said to have been successful.

People

At its heart, every organization is composed of people. People are the agents of execution. Selecting, developing, and retaining these most valuable resources is essential to success. When people possess a common problem-solving and operating framework such as Flawless Execution, they accelerate the organization to higher performance.

Altogether, the seven tiers of Flawless Execution Model can be viewed in three primary segments. The three topmost tiers, Future Picture, strategy, and leader's intent occupy the "purpose" segment. The purpose tells the organization what it intends to achieve and why.

The next segment, the center containing the Flawless Execution Cycle, is the "process" through which the organization fulfills the purpose. Finally, the bottom segment, or "platform," are those fundamental things that are essential for the process to achieve the purpose: people, training, and standards.

And that's it, a simple but comprehensive model that is essential to success. Let's turn to its single, most powerful element in the next chapter—the Stealth Debrief.

Takeaways

- We live in a complex world where predictability is impossible and cause/effect relationships are ambiguous.

- *Continuous improvement* generally refers to the *improvement of processes* rather than the improvement of organizations in a holistic way, because organizations are complex systems. It is more appropriate to say that organizations improve their performance by adapting and evolving their processes and flowing those changes into a whole that is greater than the sum of the parts.

- *Flawless Execution* is a holistic system of simple, interdependent processes that enable individuals, teams and organizations to accelerate their performance in the rapidly changing, challenging, and complex world.

- One of the most powerful tools in the Flawless Execution Cycle is the continuous improvement and learning achieved through the Stealth Debriefing process.

OPPORTUNITIES GAINED OR
OPPORTUNITIES LOST

THE FORCES OF GLOBAL change can render professional skill sets obsolete almost overnight. Companies that have been in the business of delivering coupons as a professional service have been challenged by Groupon, a company that came up with a better way. Woe be to the marketing professional who hasn't socialized the company message through Facebook or Twitter. Today's production lines look nothing like they did five years ago. Internet retailing not only became a reality but the variables that define success are also as layered and nuanced as they are customer-driven and effective. Everyone knows the wallet-opening power of a good Internet sale; Neiman-Marcus pioneered the daily, midday, Internet-only dash through the store and backed it up with a fulfillment process that delivered products to a customer's door in less than 48 hours.

> *"In principle, discussions to make revisions [debriefs] are simple: the team discusses what they expected to happen and what actually happened, explores discrepancies between expectations and reality, and adjusts their mental map accordingly."*
>
> –Donald Sull, <u>The Upside of Turbulence</u>

Organizations that fail to continuously revise assumptions about their operating environment (i.e. market) will soon face obsolescence or irrelevance. It is vital to develop the capacity to learn from your environment. The organization that does not possess formal learning structures to capture and quickly transmit key knowledge is doomed. But how do we do this? Information overload is the management crisis of the 21st century. We have so many measures, dashboards and performance indicators that acquiring information can become an end rather than a means. So let's look at knowledge. What is knowledge?

In knowledge management theory, there are two types of knowledge: explicit and tacit. *Explicit knowledge* can be written down and stored. Call that the flow of facts and figures, the data that we get when we monitor our processes, the reduction of events to statistics, and numbers, reports and instructions. For instance, for the owner of a restaurant chain, explicit knowledge would be the number of customers on a given day and at a given hour, the number of steaks sold, the number of people per table, the number of people per server, the sum of the last 100 customer service cards, the detailed step by step process for cooking a rib eye steak, the processes for opening or closing the restaurant, schedules of paid holidays, company policies, and so on. Servers the world over hum with the load of explicit knowledge and data. Diving into the nuances of those databases have created an entirely new profession of data managers.

Tacit knowledge, however, is an entirely different thing. Tacit knowledge is complex, difficult to codify, and therefore resides only in the minds of human beings. Tacit knowledge is closely related to the concepts of skill and experience.

We build our internal databases of experiences over time through our everyday interactions with the world around us. We interpret our experiences, codify our observations, pattern the behaviors that we observe, and imprint templates on our brain that have nothing to do with the mere facts and figures of a situation. Tacit knowledge involves cognition and interpretation, and conclusions that are not formulaic but may be intuitive or the result of deductive or inductive reasoning. Our inventory of tacit knowledge is thus invaluable to organizations. Tacit knowledge is the sum of our life experiences, the result of our struggle with day-to-day challenges, the products of our interactions with others, the interpretations of our observations. We innovate by drawing on our tacit knowledge. We set the tone of our organizational culture through our tacit knowledge. Call it instinct, intuition, or inspiration, tacit knowledge is to be prized.

As organizations, we want to acquire and gain from the tacit knowledge just as surely as we want our servers brimming with explicit knowledge. Of course the answer is the debrief, but let's not go there just yet. The Flawless Execution Model surrounds, of course, execution. Daily execution provides a rich opportunity for individuals to share their progress, insights, and learnings about their environment. They find out what works, what doesn't, and what new challenges or obstacles to achieving their individual tasks stand in their way—tacit knowledge.

Teamwork is at the core of knowledge sharing, but few teams are equipped with the tools to become high-performing teams. Flawless Execution helps teams and organizations both share *and* create knowledge. Amy C. Edmondson, Novartis Professor of Leadership and Management at Harvard Business School, points out that success in the new "knowledge economy" requires a focus upon "execution-as-learning."[1] For Edmondson, there are four approaches to creating such a focus: (1) use the best knowledge obtainable; (2) enable employees to collaborate; (3) routinely capture process data; and (4) study the data to find ways to improve. As a whole, the Flawless Execution model strongly supports all of these approaches. Interestingly and importantly, of these four fundamental component processes, only debriefing directly addresses all of them.

Debriefing directly links causes and effects *with* every individual involved in a project or task and, therefore, vastly increases learning experiences and also vastly improves the acquisition and spread of tacit knowledge. Now we've got explicit knowledge flowing into the company through our data portals and tacit knowledge coming in through our debriefs.

Next, we have to open the pathways that let knowledge flow across otherwise traditional and often unconscious boundaries. When lessons learned are made available to the whole organization through web-accessed databases, the inadvertent proclivity to lock learning within "stovepipes" and "silos" can be averted. As some practitioners of knowledge management have indicated, "… there is a tendency for knowledge to align itself with organizational constructs. When this is the case, learning is likely to occur in parallel—in ignorance of what another part of the organization is doing.[2] Said differently, one squadron debriefs its mission and stores its lessons learned in their silo, while another does the same thing on the other side of the country and stores their information in a different silo. No crossover, no cross-pollinating. Yet, it is precisely this sort of data that is at the core of continuous improvement. Connecting these parallel silos is one of the objectives of sharing lessons learned.

The United States Marine Corps cross-connected its stovepipes by creating the Marine Corps Lessons Learned System (MCLLS). I learned to fly in the airspace over the southern United States; not a lot of mountains and deserts in that area. But if I were a Marine deploying to Afghanistan where blowing sand and high mountains were a prominent factor, I would want to know what others had learned about that environment. Using the MCLLS, I could key in "blowing sand" and "mountainous terrain" and instantly call up a library of useful lessons learned that would increase my knowledge and capacity to excel in that new environment.

Debriefing: The Benefits

So, what are the benefits of a proper debriefing? They are numerous and fall into two categories. First, there are the discrete, tangible products that emerge directly from the debrief process. Then there are the leadership, cultural, and intangible benefits that arise from the consistent practice of debriefing.

First, debriefing formally concludes a task or project. One hears the phrase "closing the loop," and that's a good one. We bring finality to a task and move on. But not before we learn from it.

As we talked about earlier, in a complex world where predictability is impossible and innovation and risk are necessary to survive and thrive, mistakes are not only acceptable, but welcome. A healthy level of mistakes tells us that we're putting forth the extra and sometimes risky effort to succeed. Remember our fighter pilot mentality – its not a weakness to make mistakes; its weak to hide mistakes. One successful CEO put it this way: "The greatest mistake is to make no mistakes."[3]

The question then arises – through what process do we transform mistakes into innovation and adaptation? By now it should be no surprise to you that the answer is again the debrief. Data alone can't do it. Explicit knowledge falters. We have to talk to the people that were executing the plan. The objective of debriefing is to root out the mistakes and errors and stop them from recurring but also to learn from them and to innovate. Errors that emerge from incorrect assumptions help us revise those assumptions. But, errors that occur in spite of valid assumptions and proper planning must be addressed at a fundamental root cause level with both candor and sensitivity and that's where we get innovation, improvement, and problem solving once and for all. That's the process of building high-performing teams.

Debriefing provides an appropriate means of putting the past behind us, learning and growing from it, and moving on. And, when debriefing is performed regularly, it keeps the organization focused on the present and the future rather than the past. It helps us to continually revise our assumptions about the market, economy, and world.

Second, proper debriefing fulfills a critical need for effective learning by connecting cause and effect rather than allowing time delays to inhibit or prevent meaningful learning. How long can you survive the repetition of the same mistake? Bratwurst for hot dogs doesn't work if you're building a reputation for reliable party planning. What good does it do to have members of an organization contribute to a large project or planning effort and then have no connection to the outcome, no part in the post mortem? How can individuals measure themselves? Groups? Debriefing sees to it that they are intimately connected and responsible for the outcomes. Good or bad. Humans have a deep psychological need to accomplish something, to see things through. Debriefing, particularly when it is used regularly and over short time frames, helps us fulfill this need.

Third, debriefing is a catalyst for change. We've said it in several different ways, but at its heart, that's what debriefing is --- a change agent. John Kotter, the renowned scholar on change management, suggests that successful change requires management to create opportunities for 'short term wins,' thereby repetitively reinforcing positive steps along the path to change.[4] The creation of 'wins', however, presupposes an incremental process of planning in which tasks or projects are planned for and executed in relatively short periods of time. And that alone is all well and good but we'll miss the opportunity to create these short term wins unless we debrief. Consider your business. You have a sales cycle, a promotion cycle, a production cycle and so on. One may be a daily cycle, one may be weekly, and one monthly but for each process there is an inherent cycle and for each cycle there's an end point and at each end-point there should be a debrief where we tally the "wins." I fly an eight-hour mission. I debrief it immediately after I land. Not a month from now. Not after the war is over. Immediately. After a month of short term wins highlighted in my mission debriefs, I'm feeling pretty good about myself and my team and the changes we've made.

Long-range planning is, of course, important. But, plans must be broken down into smaller, shorter-range plans. Only then can one celebrate the wins and thus maintain the momentum of change, the culture of learning, the power of continuous improvement. Debriefing gives us those regular, short-term wins. Short-term wins infuse a group with confidence.

Fourth, a rigorous debriefing process seeks root causes. It is not enough to see that we had a win or a loss, rather we need to look beneath the surface to make sure it wasn't luck or some other force at work. So we ask ourselves why – why did something succeed or fail? Most of the time its obvious and we move on but not always. Air refueling is a good example of this. In the Air Force a jet flies up to a tanker and positions itself in a formation that allows a boom to reach down to a receptacle through which gas is pumped into the jet. Because the pilot of the jet had a good view of everything, it made sense to put the air refueling receptacle on the nose of his plane so he could guide the plane to the boom. As he got into formation with a tanker he could simply inch his way forward to the boom. Great line of sight, very logical, very practical.

The results were terrible. The hook-ups took far too long and the formation flying was poor. When the refueling portion of the mission was debriefed pilots complained of 'distractions' and a sense of dread that seemed out of proportion to the task itself. It was puzzling and at odds with common sense until someone threw out common sense and decided to play the 'why' game and look for a root cause by asking 'why' over and over until we got to the root cause. The 'why' they came up with was moving the refueling receptacle behind the pilot where the pilot couldn't see it at all. Why did this make sense? The group reasoned that the pilots were doing too much. They were Task Saturated. If the receptacle was out of sight, the pilot's only job would be to fly a tight formation on the tanker; it would be the boom operators job to fly the boom nozzle into the receptacle. It was transforming.

Root cause identified. Lesson learned. Today, with the exception of the A-10, most modern Air Force fighter jets are built with the refueling receptacle outside of the cone of a pilots peripheral vision. Mine was over my left shoulder. I couldn't see it. I formed on the tanker and let the boomer give me gas.

Simply looking at the obvious causes may not uncover the real forces, the 'why's.' Digging a little deeper is an essential part of a debrief. Harmful root causes can fester and grow to infect the organization if left unaddressed. Debriefing provides an opportunity to sort through the ambiguities in our complex systems and improve at the core organizational level.

Fifth, once root causes are identified, an actionable and specific lesson learned is developed. A lesson learned may require a change or amendment to existing processes, procedures, standards, rules or regulations. It may require further development of a plan or program to address the root cause. It may require a change in training or standards. Or, it may simply be a list of steps for others to utilize in future tasks and plans. Since a lesson learned is written in an explicit manner, it can be stored and made available for others in the future. Lessons learned require that an action be taken which is always assigned to a single individual who becomes responsible for implementing it.

Finally, debriefing, via the development of lessons learned, provides a rapid and simple approach to process improvement. The process called air refueling was improved after the root cause was identified and the lesson learned pumped into the system. Since debriefs occur frequently, improvement is near continuous, and results are rapidly fed into the system. We want to accelerate the learning experience, get our people up that learning curve faster, get past those first 10 missions. Debrief is about accomplishing those ends *quickly*.

> "[Wise leaders] . . . are always engaged in and by the world; they are open to 'reflective backtalk,' they can admit errors and learn from their mistakes."
>
> –Noel M. Tichy and Warren G. Bennis, Judgment:

Debriefing: Impact on Culture and Leadership

learning experience, get our people up that learning curve faster, get past those first 10 missions. Debrief is about accomplishing those ends *quickly*.

Perhaps not surprisingly, debriefing has an impact on corporate culture, too. As we've mentioned before, debriefing is a path to continuous improvement and becomes a catalyst for change. Edgar Schein, perhaps the most respected scholar on organizational culture, states that "... culture is the result of a complex group learning process."[5] Debriefing is just that, a group learning process. It is the forum in which we learn from ourselves and each other. To take charge of that process, to ritualize and develop it, is to take control of your organizational culture. The kind of culture that debriefing develops is one of learning, openness and honesty. Add to it the short-term wins and the passing of lessons learned across traditional barriers, and you see profound alignment toward executional excellence.

Debriefing also supports the development of better leaders and more cohesive teams. Debriefing requires a team leader who leads the debrief. The success of the debrief is therefore incumbent upon that leader, which in turn helps build leaders through their own trial and error. Debriefing helps build leaders by helping them learn the skills to establish greater trust between themselves and their team. Leadership is enormously complex and cannot be reduced entirely to explicit forms of knowledge. Leadership must be observed and practiced in order to be mastered. The important point, though, is that leadership can be learned.

Debriefing provides an opportunity for leadership to be developed, practiced, displayed, and observed. As you will see, the "nameless, rankless" feature of debriefing is ideally suited to developing junior executives in their careers. This comes about because of the first rule, that the planner is the debriefer; on a given mission, the junior executive may be the team leader while a senior VP may have only a supporting role. In the debrief, everyone's execution is dissected, but the meeting is led by one just person, which is invaluable leadership training. When we allow junior members to take the lead in planning and debriefing, we provide extraordinary opportunities for developing leaders.

The debrief builds greater trust between team members because of the openness and honesty demanded of all involved. When a team thoroughly discusses each other's contribution to the execution of a task, they come to know each other and understand each other's unique challenges and obstacles. Furthermore, they uncover the complexities that challenge them and learn how better to assist each other in managing those challenges.

> *"Faced with such demands, mindful organizations devote more time than other organizations to examining failure as a window on the health of the system, resisting the urge to simplify assumptions about the world."*
>
> —Weick and Sutcliffe, Managing the Unexpected

In addition to improving leaders and teams, debriefing provides insights for organization-wide improvements. Although debriefing begins at the very tactical or day-to-day operational level, the practice of debriefing should cascade upward in the organization. For an organization as a whole, the analysis of recurring root causes is a powerful tool of continuous improvement. Such analysis provides a capacity to identify or self-diagnose a host of organizational weaknesses. Of course, because deep-seated organizational shortcomings may be obscured by complexity, a system for categorizing common issues must be utilized. Later, we'll discuss just such a comprehensive system for the classification of root causes in every debrief.

Finally, debriefing is a central component to developing a culture of *high reliability*. Scholars and researchers have closely studied why some complex organizations in high-risk environments have operated with very few accidents over many years. These organizations have been labeled High-Reliability Organizations (HROs). Karl Weick and Kathleen Sutcliffe published their findings in *Managing the Unexpected*. In it, the authors note that high-risk operations like air traffic control, aircraft carriers, and nuclear power plants display these characteristics. For example, aircraft carrier flight operations demonstrate slightly less than three fatalities per 100,000 flight hours in an extremely hostile, unforgiving, and constantly-changing environment.

Overall, Weick and Sutcliffe have coined the term *mindfulness* to describe five characteristics of most HROs. Of those five characteristics, three are directly supported by debriefing practices. According to Weick and Sutcliffe:

1. HROs appear to be preoccupied with failure of all sizes and shapes. They do not dismiss small deviations or settle on narrow, localized explanations of these problems. They treat each small failure as a potential indication of a much larger problem.[6] For HROs, "the only problem is a hidden one." Root cause analysis within proper debriefing processes and techniques seeks out those recurring root causes, in order for the organization to address them.

2. HROs exhibit a reluctance to simplify interpretations. HROs recognize that humans tend to oversimplify the world, so they try to resist that tendency. They look for odd things that don't seem to fit their picture of how things usually work. They build diverse teams and welcome a wide variety of perspectives to challenge conventional wisdom.[7] The Stealth Debrief process that will be introduced in the next chapter encourages an environment for participants to be unsatisfied with simple answers. Furthermore, it allows the participants to raise their concerns in a psychologically safe environment where their opinion is valued.

3. HROs demonstrate a commitment to resilience. They recognize that no hazardous and complex system will be error free. They recognize that mistakes happen, but are not typically due to negligence or malfeasance. For HROs, mistakes often suggest systemic problems.[8] The Stealth Debrief process creates a forum where participants can accept failures and learn from them in a positive, non-attributive manner while relentlessly seeking root causes and systemic issues. Remember, Flawless Execution is not about executing flawlessly, but the endless *pursuit* of flawless execution.

A Final Word on Learning

The events of the past few years have seen the decline and fall of many businesses, large and small. The economic earthquake of 2008 exposed the learning gaps within organizations, gaps that, for many, became fatal wounds. Business guru and author Jim Collins reviewed the root causes behind many of these failures and offered suggestions to prevent such failures. Of those suggestions, he recommends "blameless autopsies" (debriefs) and cultivating an ability to accept full responsibility and learn from mistakes.[9]

As a learning tool, debriefing is essential. We live in a world of rapid change that we have no real capacity to predict. What we learn today may save us tomorrow. Knowledge is perishable; it requires institutionalized debriefing to keep it fresh and up to date. Those organizations that hold debriefing as a "sacred" part of their culture, thrive.

Takeaways

Tangible Benefits of Debriefing

- Debriefing formally concludes a task or project, closes the loop, and allows the team to move on.

- Debriefing provides an essential change management tool by providing a forum to celebrate short-term wins, one of John Kotter's eight steps of leading change.

- A rigorous debriefing process seeks root causes of those wins (and losses).

- Debriefs produce actionable and specific lessons learned.

- Debriefing provides a rapid and simple approach to process improvement.

Cultural and Leadership Benefits of Debriefing

- Debriefing helps develop an organizational culture of learning, openness and honesty.

- Debriefing supports the development of better leaders and more cohesive teams.

- Debriefing provides insights for organization-wide improvements.

- Debriefing is a central component to developing the culture of a High-Reliability Organization (HRO).

THE STEALTH DEBRIEF

THE FIRST QUESTION WE hear when we introduce the Stealth Debrief is the "what" question. What constitutes an event of sufficient importance for a debrief? Good question. Remember that a debrief follows the execution of a plan, so we're really asking ourselves what constitutes an event sufficient to brief a specific plan and debrief the outcomes.

Since it provides an opportunity to reflect on *what* has happened and *why,* a debrief should follow any significant and even unexpected event. The frequency of debriefing can vary by industry and corporation. In every work environment there are natural cycles. In retail and in the food service sectors there are finite operating hours—the store opening and the store closing—just as there is the opening bell and the closing bell in the finance sector. In these sectors, and in the hospitality sector as well, the daily variances may be too insignificant to have daily plans and debriefs, but a weekly plan and weekly debriefing with the service staff would seem essential.

Processes have their own cycles, too. In a consumer packaged goods company, marketing is an ongoing process but events are staggered across a timeline and special events take on special significance. Because change is so nearly instantaneous and almost always unpredictable, we like weekly plans and weekly debriefings of even inside processes that may ordinarily have a monthly or quarterly planning cycle.

Events are always bookended by plans at the start and debriefs at the end, with interim debriefs or focused meetings scheduled to keep the team on task. An event may be a new product launch, a major football promotion, an unexpected weather phenomena, major sales calls, major presentations, and so on. Any plan or activity that requires a *group* to execute it is always preceded by a statement of the plan and concluded with a debrief. We like to call these plans and projects *missions.*

As if it's not obvious by now, for all other situations, a week is about as long as our clients feel comfortable going without holding department or team meetings.

The Stealth acronym was created to help you easily remember the seven sequential steps of an effective debrief. By way of a brief overview, here are those parts.

S – Set the Time; Debriefing should be part of the plan, project, or mission
T – Tone; Nameless and rankless
E – Execution vs. Objectives; Review the execution and determine the results—the successes and errors
A – Analyze Execution; Seek root causes for each success and error
L – Lesson Learned; Clear and precise
T – Transfer Lesson Learned; Transmit and store
H – High Note; End with a positive summary

Now, in more detail:

- **S - Set Time** – Before you begin your mission, determine the location, start time and end time of the debrief. The debrief is part of the mission. Schedule the debrief immediately following the end of the project, plan or mission. "Immediately" may be the next business day, but it does not mean the next week. Debriefs begin exactly on time and, as a rule of thumb, should last no more than an hour.

- **T - Tone** – Nameless and rankless debrief. This means that anyone can bring up any issue without fear of reprimand. It's an issue of trust. This tone is set by having the leader start with his or her own mistakes. Even in the case of perfect results, the leader may want to point out any "near misses" that might have led to shortfalls. This creates the kind of open communication that gets to the important issues and avoids the blame game so common in organizations.

- **E - Execution versus Objectives** – Now that the team is communicating openly, it's time to review the execution of the mission at hand. Repeat the mission objective and compare results to that objective. Present the original plan and list the results, successes and errors.

- **A - Analyze Execution** – Determine the direct causes of the successes and errors in the execution. "Cause = *How* did it happen?" Then dive deeper to determine their root causes. "*Why, why, why …?*"

- **L - Lessons Learned** – This is where the debriefing team takes the prominent or recurring root causes from the previous step and turns them into critical step-by-step actions that can be used to improve future mission planning.

- **T - Transfer Lessons Learned** – Communicate lessons learned throughout the organization. Who needs this lesson, how fast, and how will we get it to them? This is how debriefing accelerates the experience of the entire organization by allowing others to learn from the experience of a few. Learning from our past informs and improves future execution.

- **H - High Note** – End the debrief on a high note. Positively summarize the accomplishments of the plan or project. After dissecting the mission, admitting errors and underscoring successes, end the debrief by summarizing the successes. The team should leave the debrief with a positive sense of accomplishment.

Before detailing the steps in the Stealth Debrief, there are a few questions to answer. Foremost: Who does what in a debrief, and whose attendance is mandatory?

Every mission has a leader and it is the leader's responsibility to develop the plan. However, in the military as in civilian life, a leader may not be the most senior person on the team. It was often the case that a captain would be the leader of a four-ship of F-15s, with a colonel or even a general flying as a wingman. The same is true in business; the head of government affairs may be the project leader, but the team's performance may heavily rely on the performance of the VP of Communication.

The plan comes about by drawing on the resources at hand and includes a list of tasks, or course of action, plus contingencies. The leader prepares the final plan and then briefs it to the team. Questions are answered, and a team-wide final agreement ends the brief.

After the mission, the leader is back on stage for the debrief. Here are the mandatory items:

- Attendance is mandatory. If you were part of the mission, you're a part of the debrief.

- The lead planner always leads the debrief.

- Outsiders, those not involved with the plan or its execution, are not allowed to attend.

- We leave name and rank at the door.

- Disciplinary issues involving individuals are never raised or addressed in a debrief.

The Seven Steps: By the Book

Step 1: Set the Time

The debrief is part of the mission. The timeline for the mission includes the time set aside for the debrief. Thus, the debrief is considered to be an essential part of the plan itself and no mission is complete until the debrief is complete. In the best case, the debrief should be held immediately following a mission and, in the worst case, no more than a week later. Scheduling a debrief means setting aside a specific place and time. There should be no uncertainty about where and when it will be held.

A debrief is conducted by the appointed leader of the plan, project, or mission. Unless a professional facilitator is conducting the debrief for training purposes, no one should stand in for the responsible leader except under the most extreme circumstances. The leader sets the tone for the debrief and accepts responsibility for both the project plan and the outcome of the debrief.

Debriefs start on time and end on time. No one comes in late; no one leaves early. The rigid nature of this rule is to implicitly communicate that a debrief is serious business and a corporate imperative.

A proper debrief will be as intense as it is candid; therefore it can't go on for long and remain productive. An hour should be sufficient.

Be smart. No cell phones or Blackberrys. No interruptions.

Step 2: Tone

> "*When you conduct autopsies without blame, you go a long way toward creating a climate where the truth is heard. If you have the right people on the bus, you should almost never need to assign blame but need only to search for understanding and learning.*"
>
> –Jim Collins, <u>Good To Great</u>

The proper tone is the most difficult and the most significant attribute of a debrief. Our objective is to have a meeting that is disciplined, psychologically safe, and honest. We want the team to feel free of judgment. We know it's a weakness to hide mistakes. The first steps to that end is the setting.

Debriefing is not a spectator sport. To draw out the best information, the concise thinking, the root cause analysis, a participant can't feel as if they're on display for outsiders to watch and judge. People admit mistakes and provide constructive criticism when they're among their peers – those with a vested interest in the project. Debriefs are held in places safe from prying eyes, outside distractions and interruptions – a closed-door conference room with no windows, for example. In fact, it is best to hold debriefs in the same location time after time. When the debriefing location is consistent, then the location itself will serve to perpetuate the appropriate tone. That location becomes a sanctuary for debriefing. Holding debriefs in the same place reinforces the sense of psychological safety and the discipline necessary to carry it out successfully.

Next, we only allow those on the mission to be in the room. Been there, done that, saw it first hand. The mission was a shared experience. If they didn't share in it, they're not in the room. If they did, its mandatory to attend no matter how minor their contribution.

Third, it's always nameless and rankless. On our flight suits back in the 1980's, our name tags and rank are affixed with Velcro patches. We would literally or figuratively peel them off and throw them in a bucket as we enter the room. My name is no longer Jim Murphy, I am no longer a Captain. I am "2", which was my position in the formation. A critique of me might be, "2, you were flying 500 feet in line abreast instead of the briefed one-mile spread formation as we entered the combat area." Not Jim Murphy. Not captain Murphy. Not a personal attack on me.

Fourth, the team leader starts the meeting and always starts with truthful self-criticism. It's the leader's responsibility to ensure the nameless, rankless, and trusting tone of the debrief. No flight is flawless but this opening is not about something trivial. The deeper the leader digs into his soul, the more truth will follow as the comments go around the table.

Psychological safety – that's the key. For learning experiences to be positive, the learner must feel that the learning environment is psychologically safe.[1] In other words, they must feel comfortable making and admitting mistakes to the group. The need for that safety has long been recognized in the fighter-pilot culture. There are no points for second place, and that's for good reason. Pilot's understand that they contribute to the safety and success of their team mates and that's why they feel safe in their debriefs. There's a level of respect for each other and a level of respect for the consequences of mistakes. We want to create that environment in the business debrief. The leader makes sure that every "pilot" in the business debrief has their say and is given their due. As the debrief settles in, a level of respect suffuses the room. A Senior VP becomes intensely interested in the perspectives of a 26-year-old business school graduate if for no other reason than he or she has to rely on that person if that Senior VP wants to continue the upward trajectory of his or her own career.

The effect of leadership upon the success of a debrief cannot be overemphasized. Good leaders possess courage and integrity. No leader can demonstrate integrity and courage better than by admitting their own mistakes. A leader that is always "right" can squelch opinion and constructive criticism. This act of admitting one's own mistakes first is often called *inside-outside criticism*. We internalize the criticism by looking inward first. Only after such inside criticism can we turn criticism outward to external events.

A good leader cannot be above criticism. Even if a leader has a good plan with the right answers, it does not mean that someone else cannot help make a better plan with better answers. That is why the most significant step a leader can take to set a tone of safety and honesty in a debrief is by admitting their own mistakes first. And then they should open the discussion for others to critique them. "Did anyone else see me do anything dumb, different from what we briefed, or dangerous?" Their humility will lead others to do the same. The mantra for every organization should be *"It's not who's right. It's what's right."*

Step 3: Execution vs. Objectives

Once the proper tone has been set, the first order of business is reviewing the objective. The team needs to assess how it executed according to its mission objective. Our example objective was to host a companywide picnic for all 48 employees, offering up a hot dogs-

and-softball day with tubs of cola and beer. If, at that point, one of the team members did not clearly understand the mission objective, then a root cause for failure may have been identified already. That objective should be restated so the entire team knows exactly what the objective was, in order to measure its success.

A review here is in order. We've talked about plans and planning and having a clear Future Picture of where you want to go, your objective. In Flawless Execution, this is the first step in planning: We develop a clear, measureable, and achievable objective that supports the Future Picture. Once we have the objective, we develop the plan and brief the group. When we come back, the first question we ask is, "Was the objective met?" Since the mission objective had to be measurable, the immediate answer will be a clear yes or no. However, we must go deeper than that. Even if the mission was successful, there are often smaller errors or issues that could have contributed to a larger failure, which in turn could indicate deep issues that need to be addressed. So we look at each element of the plan to see what actually happened.

The team needs to agree upon how the objective and the specific tasks within the planned course of action varied from the actual execution. In other words, what was done differently from the plan? If the team said they were going to do a specific list of tasks—someone will get the hot dogs, another will get the beer, and a third the condiments—did they omit those tasks or did they perform them differently than originally planned? From that simple analysis, the team can identify the significant successes and errors from each step. We call that list the *results*. Results are those things that warrant further review and, potentially, a root cause analysis. We'll take a closer look at the process of identifying results in the next chapter. As a rule of thumb, keep this results list to six to eight items. More than 10 items indicates that your group could be mired in unproductive hair-splitting.

Step 4: Analyze Execution.

Once the team has created a list of results, it's time to analyze each in turn. The team takes the first result and asks, "How did this happen?" The answer may or may not be obvious; some discussion may be required. It is important not to make assumptions. The team should only simply answer how the success or error occurred—specifically what precipitated the result. These causes will generally be specific to some action or omission traced to an individual, or to an influence external to the team. Once the direct cause is established, the team can determine the root cause.

A debriefing technique employed by the U.S. Navy's Blue Angels flight demonstration squadron is to review each individual's performance, starting with the leader, following every performance. Instead of reviewing every turn and pass by each pilot, they progress in round-robin style from one pilot to the next. Each admits their errors, then opens the discussion for others to provide additional comments. Once all the errors are on the table, the pilot says, "I've made these mistakes and I'm going to fix them." This is a powerful statement for several reasons. First, it lets everyone on the team know that the individual pilot is conscious of the mistake and is willing to address it. Second, it builds greater trust among the team as a whole because each member demonstrates full responsibility for their actions and behaviors. Finally, it forms the basis for the open and honest dialogue that is so critical to spotting and correcting small errors before they cascade into larger ones.

These candid discussions keep errors close to the root causes. For teams like the Blue Angels, where small errors left unchecked can rapidly grow into catastrophic failures, root causes must always be thoroughly sought. Root causes are not part of the common language of business, and therefore are difficult to classify.

Using our Flawless Execution Model, root causes are defined and categorized very specifically. Altogether, there are 21 general root cause errors within four categories. A matrix of these root causes can be found in <u>Table 1</u>. Later we will look at these 21 root causes in more detail.

Root Causes Matrix			
Core	Planning	Team	Execution
People	Objective	Leadership	Task Saturation
Training	Threats	Organization	Crosschecks
Standards	Resources	Communication	Mutual Support
Strategy	Lessons Learned	Knowledge	Checklists
Vision	Course of Action	Experience	X-Gap
	Contingencies	Discipline	

Table 1

Failures can be the result of "stupid humans," while successes can be the result of lone, courageous heroes. But Flawless Execution is about improving organizational excellence and determining what processes or systems need to be improved to prevent errors in the future. Organizations that develop high-performing cultures minimize such errors. In Flawlessly Executing cultures, the whole is greater than the sum of its parts. That is, individuals work together as a cooperative whole to accelerate each other's performance. Unfortunately, many organizations never become more than a collection of individuals. They never become high-performing teams.

Root cause analysis begins by thinking about causes outside or beyond those of the individual. For example, assume that someone on the team made a mistake. Was there an opportunity for one of their teammates to notice the potential for failure and help them out? Were they Task Saturated because of too much to do and too little time to do it? Was the objective really achievable, given the available time and resources? Are the organizational standards that govern processes outdated or inadequate? Is the organization hiring the right people and training them properly?

Look beyond the individual and toward root causes in the systems and processes that support the individual.

> *"In many organizations, it is extremely difficult to institutionalize time for reflection and continuous learning. . . . But in our experience, creating and maintaining time for checking in with people, teasing out the lessons of recent experiences, and sharing those lessons widely in the organization is critical to adaptability in a changing world."*
>
> –Heifetz, Grashow and Linsky, <u>The Practice of Adaptive Leadership</u>

Step 5: Lessons Learned

A lesson learned succinctly and clearly states the action that a team will take in the future to repeat successes and avoid errors under similar situations. Lessons learned are never vague. For example, "communicate better" is not a workable lesson learned, because it does not specify an action that a future team can take to address the same or similar objectives.

A lesson learned, of course, must be actionable. To ensure that the action is carried out, a specific individual is assigned that responsibility during the debrief. This person is indicated as the Specific Point of Accountability (SPA). The date or timeline by which action or transfer should be completed is also assigned prior to the conclusion of the debrief.

Step 6: Transfer Knowledge

The next question is, "Okay, great, I have a lesson learned, but how do we transfer it so that others may benefit from it?" First of all, members of the debrief will have learned the lesson in the most effective way, by experiencing it firsthand. Now we need to transform that tacit knowledge into explicit knowledge, so it can be promulgated throughout the organization.

Once you have a number of individuals who have firsthand experience and an organized and accessible means of retrieving the written lesson learned, you must make sure that you connect these two sources of learning by developing the right kind of context and references. Doing so requires some further activity on the part of the debrief team. A properly documented lesson learned contains more information than the lesson learned alone. It contains a reference to the mission plan that was debriefed, the result, the cause, the root cause, the accountable SPA, and the timeline. This gives context and references to anyone who may need to utilize the lesson learned in the future. The SPA provides a single contact for more information on the lesson learned or mission. Finally, such context provides information that will help others assess whether the lesson learned remains relevant as time passes.

The key to transferring the lesson learned is determining whether the lesson should be "pushed" or "pulled." Ask the following questions: "Who needs this lesson? How fast do they need it? How should we get it to them?" Some lessons learned need to get to certain people immediately, and some need to get to everyone in a timely fashion. Such lessons need to be "pushed." Perhaps they can be communicated by telephone or e-mail. They may even be so important as to merit a meeting or video teleconference.

Many corporations and government organizations have large databases of lessons learned that are easily accessed via a web interface. The United States Marine Corps and the National Aeronautical and Space Administration (NASA) are two large organizations that have derived great benefits from lessons learned databases. In electronic databases, users may simply type in a few keywords to generate a list of lessons that may be relevant to whatever plan is being developed. Smaller organizations might have simple paper filing systems for their databases, or simply place them in a searchable electronic file.

Of course, over time files and databases of lessons learned will grow. Some lessons will become outdated or irrelevant. To keep lessons relevant and useful, every organization can establish a process in which lessons are reviewed for relevancy and archived. This simple process will also provide the opportunity to combine some related lessons learned.

Step 7: End on a High Note

Don't dwell on the negative. Years of experience with military fighter pilots prove the power of ending debriefs on a positive note. Always find the success in a mission, no matter how small, and end the debrief positively no matter how limited the mission's success may have been. It is critical that the team leave the debrief with their dignity intact. Always end with positive encouragement and personal thanks for what the team did right. Don't go back at the end and summarize all the results; end on a positive note. Remember, debriefs should never be punitive or negative. Once they become viewed as such, they will cease to be useful.

Last, what happens in the debrief stays in the debrief. The only products of a debrief are the record that includes the lesson learned and the tacit knowledge and experience gained by each participant.

One note to remember: The first debrief can be awkward. People are new to this. They're uncomfortable with the concept. They think things went well, so why debrief? Again, we come from a culture of planning, not debriefing. Stick to your guns. The first one may indeed be awkward, but you'll get through it.

One final but very important note about the debriefing: In a mature organization that frequently practices the Stealth Debrief, simply making the statement, "Let's debrief" carries with it all the sanctity of the tone introduced in this chapter and all the processes to follow in the remainder of this book. The word "debrief" carries with it the sense of opportunity and an eagerness to learn.

Takeaways

The Stealth Debrief process is the most comprehensive and effective method for debriefing. It includes the following steps:

S – Set the Time; Debriefing should be part of the plan, project, or mission

T – Tone; Nameless and rankless

E – Execution vs. Objectives;

A – Analyze Execution; Seek root causes

L – Lesson Learned; Clear and precise

T – Transfer Lesson Learned; Transmit and store

H – High Note; End with a positive summary

Guidelines for Proper Debriefing:

- A debrief will not be successful without a clearly articulated mission objective.

- The mission is not complete until the debrief is complete.

- Hold the debrief within 1 week of the completion of a plan, project, mission or course of action.

- Only the responsible and accountable leader of the plan, project or mission conducts the debrief.

- Debriefs begin exactly on time and last no more than 1 hour.

- Celebrate successes after the debrief is complete.

- Outsiders, those not involved with the plan, project or mission, are not allowed to attend.

- Disciplinary issues involving individuals should never be addressed in a debrief.

- Establish an actionable lesson learned with specific accountability and a timeline for completion.

- Determine whether a lesson learned should be "pushed" or "pulled" information, and transfer it accordingly.

- Set up a process to periodically review lessons learned for relevancy.

THE ISSUE OF EFFECTIVENESS

RESULTS ARE THE "MEAT and potatoes" of the debrief, the raw material of analysis. What caused the mission to fail? –Number 2 aircraft overflew the target. What caused the product to fail to ship on time? – Manufacturing couldn't produce the quantity we ordered. What accounts for a doubling of our anticipated profit? –The sales force penetrated a major new market segment. We're not asking *why* those things happened yet; we're just asking what went wrong and what went right. Next to setting the right tone, reaching consensus on results is one of the most vitally important components of debriefing. That's because the results relate to the effectiveness of the plan and its execution.

What the finance department plans to do today or what the research and development department plans to do tomorrow isn't really relevant to the organization's Future Picture unless, in even some small way, those plans help to realize that Future Picture. That's the issue of effectiveness. Is what we're doing really impactful? Are we being effective? That's not always easy to answer. We get caught up in the tactics. Short-range objectives should contribute to the bigger, long-range ones. Our tactics should support the strategy. That's fundamental to any aligned organization.

What I've discovered from a lot of clients is that, in planning and executing, people get caught up in the details and forget the big picture. They miss the forest for the trees. Debriefing is what we all need to stay aligned.

For example, a good friend and client, someone who has been debriefing to the Stealth Model for more than 15 years, just recently rediscovered how important it is to focus on effectiveness in the debrief. He volunteered to assist a nonprofit organization in putting on a series of fundraising events. They planned every detail: the food, the signage, the greeters at every entrance to the facility, even down to the seven planned stage announcements and the script for each of those announcements. The 21 people who helped plan and execute that event were ecstatic at the end of the program. Consensus was that it just could not have been more perfectly executed.

Though my friend was experienced in conducting debriefs, and one of the organization's leaders was a former fighter pilot, they were reluctant to hold a debrief with the other 19 team members. Those other folks had never debriefed before and, with the perceived success of the program, why debrief perfection, right? But my friend and his former fighter pilot team member insisted, and it's a good thing they did. When they got to Step Three, Analyze Execution, they took each task in turn and asked the team whether it was effective. Everything was a "yes" until they got to the task that addressed the seven planned announcements. There, they uncovered a major error and actually learned something about a motivation that no one had yet articulated. This was a nonprofit organization in need of donations and membership, and not once during all seven planned announcements, nor at any other point in the program, did the planners provide membership information to any of the guests.

This is a valuable by-product of the debrief. The team executed their plans perfectly, but no one had articulated "grow the organization's membership" as part of the objective. The event was a success by the objectives they had established—attendance and smooth coordination during the event—but a measure of success could have been "new members" or "donations." They had all talked about it. They spruced up the event facility and made it sparkle. But in the debrief they realized that they had become consumed by the details of executing the event and lost sight of memberships. This was a tremendous "aha" moment. Everything had been perfect— but, well, not really. It was an invaluable lesson learned. The good news is that they fixed it. Two weeks later, when the second event was held, those announcements contained explicit details on how to apply for membership and every guest got a card in their gift bags explaining the same process and why their membership was important.

In Flawless Execution, we say that the objectives of any plan or mission should be four things: clear, measureable, achievable, and support the Future Picture. If an objective doesn't support the Future Picture, then why are we doing it? The lessons the nonprofit group learned: Don't get caught up in the tactics, however perfectly you may execute them; and never, ever assume you did a great job until you debrief.

And that's the crux of identifying the results in Step Three of the Stealth Debrief. You must review your plan in detail and assess its individual task effectiveness. Until you do that, you can only make assumptions about the real results.

Identifying results, and then analyzing those results for their causes and root causes, is an art—not a science. We live and work in a world dominated by a high level of complexity that obscures our capacity to clearly identify cause and effect. That's the proverbial "fog of war," where confusion inevitably arises from the execution of most any plan. As an often-quoted military maxim purports, no plan survives first contact with the enemy. But, as with any art, practice improves our ability to sort through it all and make some sense of it. Agreeing on results is the first step in sorting through that ambiguity.

To begin isolating the results, start with a simple framework of three questions. (1) Did we execute as planned? (2) Were the individual tasks within the plan effective? (3) Overall, what went wrong?

First, come to agreement on whether the plan was executed as briefed (assuming you planned and briefed in the first place). In other words, did we do what we planned to do? If the answer is no, then seek out those tasks that were not executed as planned. Tasks that varied from the plan would then become the first results to note. Even if the plan was executed as it was briefed, an analysis of each step may still yield valuable insight, as my friend discovered. We often encounter unexpected challenges or uncover new knowledge, even in the simplest tasks. If the debriefing does not present an opportunity to capture that information and learning, then it will most likely be lost. Even successful plans should be reviewed task by task.

Identifying Results Framework
1. Did we execute as planned?   2. Were the individual tasks within the plan *effective*?   3. Overall, what went wrong?

Second, take the plan task by task and ask, "Was this task *effective*?" We might successfully complete a task without having any positive effect upon the objective. Similarly, we might fail to perform a task and yet create no negative effect upon the overall success of the mission objective at all. But asking whether a task was effective directs the team to analyze the results to a much deeper and more qualitative level. If my task was to strike the target with a GBU-16 thousand-pound laser-guided bomb and I did so, then my task was successful. But was it effective? Perhaps not, if it failed to penetrate the hardened bunker and take out the command center inside. Did you successfully make 50 cold calls every day? Yes, but were they effective? Asking about the *effectiveness* rather than the success of a task prompts a more evaluative discussion that can uncover valuable learning and details for significant adaptations and adjustments. That learning should be captured as results in the debrief.

Often, a team will debrief a mission, but the reason for success or failure may not be clearly attributed to any specific task. However, the team may have perceptions or recall clues that indicate what task or collection of tasks contributed to the final outcome. So the third question helps us step back from looking at the individual trees and take in the whole forest.

After dissecting the effectiveness of the individual tasks within the plan, the team needs to ask what went wrong. This final question may seem superfluous, but as often happens, the tasks within a plan may appear to have had little bearing on the ultimate success or failure of the plan. A team might meet with success in spite of making many mistakes. It may also fail to accomplish the plan's objective in spite of flawlessly executing every task. That is just the ambiguity that the process of identifying results must cut through. By taking a step back from the details and asking, overall, *What went wrong? What do we need to take a closer look at?*, we may bring greater clarity to identifying ambiguous results.

One common example of such ambiguity is in sales. A sales team may plan and execute a sales presentation superbly, yet still not make the sale. Take a look at Appendix C, which demonstrates how to identify results with this simple three-question framework when faced with such ambiguity.

To identify the results, though, does not identify the underlying root causes. Only by identifying and addressing the root causes can organizations improve on a fundamental level. Like treating the symptoms rather than the disease, addressing causes rather than root causes only serves to hide systemic weaknesses.

This chapter addressed the ambiguities of analysis of the "E" in Stealth Debriefing: Execution versus Objectives. The next chapter dives deeper into that process of analysis by seeking out and categorizing root causes in the "A," or Analyze Execution step.

Takeaways

To aid in the identification of results, ask the following sequence of questions:

1. Did we execute as planned?
2. Were the individual tasks within the plan effective?
3. Overall, what went wrong?

ROOT CAUSE ANALYSIS

BECAUSE ROOT CAUSES CAN be so deeply ingrained in an organization, root cause analysis is a difficult task to undertake. The debriefing team needs to dig deep to find underlying causes which may be both ambiguous and numerous.

We perform root cause analysis by taking the list of results developed in Step Three and subjecting each result to a relentless assault of "why's." We keep asking why this particular result happened until we get to the root cause, the real problem.

Because every company is unique there is no one-size-fits-all template but there are four common categories that usually are responsible, one of which may fit the bill for the overwhelming majority of your problems.

They are:

1. Core
2. Planning
3. Team
4. Execution

Root Causes Category 1: Core

People

At the most fundamental level, an organization cannot exist without people. People are the foundational tier of the Flawless Execution Model. As many business and organizational management gurus have indicated, organizations must get the "right" people onboard. That means hiring people with the right personality traits and values, in addition to the right knowledge, skills and abilities.

Citing people as individuals is NOT the intent of this category. The purpose of the People category is to isolate *root causes that influence the overall talent pool*. Hence, HR functions predominate in this category. Citing "people" as a root cause could include issues such as hiring and screening practices, employment policies, or labor resources in the local area.

Training

The objective of training is to develop the knowledge and skills necessary to properly execute a plan. If training was available but a key team member was not properly trained, this is a root cause. Thus, root causes categorized as "training deficiency" are those issues in which training was available but not utilized. A caveat to this is illustrated by a test pilot. A test pilot may crash a plane, but training would not be a root cause because there is no specific set of training manuals for the experimental aircraft.

Every new plan, project or mission provides an opportunity to identify training needs. The objective of training is to develop the knowledge and skills necessary to execute properly. Thus, root causes involving training should only be those in which training *should have been available and utilized* in order to fulfill knowledge gaps for known or anticipated needs. Training cannot address the unknown; so do not cite training as an error if its need could *not* have been anticipated.

Also, do not confuse training with education. Generally speaking, training addresses known challenges while education is a resource we draw upon to address unknown or new challenges. Training addresses specific needs to accomplish specific tasks. If education appears to be a cause of error or success, then consider this a root cause that falls within the People category.

Standards

Standards refer to written guidance that provides a minimum level of execution. Failures that fall in this category call into question the veracity or applicability of the standard or process in question, and whether revision or replacement of the standard process is required. Most commonly, lessons learned addressing root causes in this category require revisions of existing standards or drafting of new standards.

We've discussed several instances of standards as they apply to training. For example, the Strategic Air Command required a perfect score on its pilot assessment and, as a fighter pilot, I was allowed only two opportunities to correct a mistake. Those are standards. Failure of a standard calls into question its effectiveness and asks whether the standard needs revision.

Strategy

It could be that a strategy was wrong. The outcomes of all good plans have a simple litmus test: they should be clear, measureable, achievable, and support the achievement of the organization's Future Picture. If a strategy does not do any one of these four things, then the strategy was flawed and it becomes a root cause. My objective may be to increase my market share 25%, and one of my strategies may be to decrease my price by 5%. That seems logical until we debrief the plan and see that market share actually declined. What happened? We did everything according to plan, including our pricing strategy. In our root cause analysis, someone brings it to our attention that competitors dropped their prices 30%, thus rendering null not only our own price decrease but causing our plan to fail.

Future Picture

Like a strategy, an organization's Future Picture could be at fault. Consider the picnic. The Future Picture has to be detailed and specific. Was it clear enough? Was it actionable? Was it detailed enough to provide guidance across the entire range of processes within the organization? The idea of a war on terror is pretty specific, but denying the Taliban bases in Pakistan and Afghanistan is detailed and actionable. A Future Picture is different from a strategy in that it should be highly defined and thoroughly describe the future aspirations of the organization in a variety of different facets or aspects. The Future Picture should be the goal-setting statement for the entire organization. Citing the Future Picture as a root cause says that it is either based upon incorrect assumptions or that it is not adequately defined.

Root Causes Category 2: Planning

There are six possible root causes that fall under the category of planning. Each corresponds to one of the six steps in planning that is part of the Flawless Execution Cycle.

Objective

If the objective is not properly formulated, the entire plan may be doomed to failure. Again, objectives must be clear, measureable, achievable and support the organization's overall Future Picture. Plans that support the execution of the strategic plan have what we call clear line-of-sight to the objective. Line-of-sight alignment means that those executing the plan clearly understand how the plan supports the objective. Good line-of-sight allows team members to exercise judgment when things go wrong by providing clear guidance toward the ultimate desired outcome or effect. Hot dogs and softball? I don't see any mustard on the condiments table. I know what needs to be done. That's clear line-of-sight against a clear, measureable objective.

Objectives must be *clear* in the sense that they can be simply stated in written form without ambiguous language. They must be *measurable* in that real, tangible and objective evidence exists to prove success has been achieved at a specific point in time. And they should be *achievable*. Objectives can be challenging, but they must not be perceived as too difficult or impossible to achieve by the team.

Threats

Once an objective has been crafted, the planning team identifies the threats to its accomplishment. Planning efforts that fail to make a concerted effort to identify potential obstacles foolishly ignore the harsh realities of the world. Teams cannot anticipate all eventualities, and no success is ever guaranteed. But teams can, at least, identify the obvious dangers and uncertainties, the "known unknowns."

Resources

What resources are required to execute the mission? How can we negate, mitigate or avoid the threats we've identified? Whether it is money, talent, time, etc., planners often fail to ask for what they really need. Once you map out the threats to a specific mission objective, you will likely find that you either have, or have access to, adequate resources to meet most threats.

An important aspect to note about both Threats and Resources in the context of planning is that together, these two components of planning constitute basic risk assessment. Are sufficient resources available to accomplish the mission? If not, is your objective really achievable?

Lessons Learned

Did we make a mistake another team already made? Where are those lessons learned? Why did we get defeated by something others had already identified? Good planning starts with lessons learned. You never plan in a vacuum. Seek the experience and advice of everyone on the planning team and anyone else outside the planning team that may have relevant experience. For teams and organizations that regularly conduct debriefs and transfer learning, consult the lessons learned databases. Finally, brainstorm among the individuals within the planning team for insight into related experiences that might aid in the development of a better plan.

> *"Many conclude that it borders on dereliction that their organizations invest so few resources in studying what has succeeded and failed in their past strategies . . ."*
>
> –Peter M. Senge, The Fifth Discipline

Course of Action

Who, what and when? These are the elements of a plan's course-of action (COA). Every plan has a COA ... but maybe that was the problem. Every task within a good course of action has at least three components. The task should indicate *who* will do *what* and *when*. Specifically, the COA must be clearly written and indicate the specific individual responsible for performing the task, what the task is, and when it will be performed or completed. We said we would have mustard and ketchup at the picnic, but we didn't assign any one person the responsibility to get the condiments.

A good way to improve a plan is to *Red Team* the plan. Because we all fall in love with our own plans, we Red Team a plan by bringing in an outside group and asking them to take a look at our objective and course of action and openly criticize it. The Red Team should tell us what they think is wrong and what we forgot to consider. A good Red Team exposes the flaws of a plan so the planning team can address them and improve the plan before it is executed.

Contingency Plan

What if it rains? What do I do with a company picnic that centers on softball? Every good plan should consider what could go wrong and plan for such contingencies. Contingency plans should have clear triggers. Triggers are specific events or indicators that unambiguously indicate to the team that the contingency plan must be put into effect. Rain is a unambiguous indicator that we're not going to play softball and it's time for Plan B.

Root Causes Category 3: Team

Here we find a set of root causes related to the elements found in high-performing teams, what we like to call L.O.C.K.E.D. or "Locked on Teams." LOCKED is an acronym for those six elements—leadership, organization, communication, knowledge, experience, and discipline—that enable high-performing teams to succeed.

Leadership

Of all the root causes, leadership has the greatest effect upon success or failure. Leadership affects every aspect of an organization for good or ill.

For the purpose of categorizing root cause analysis, leadership deals with developing the team, aligning the team toward the objective and holding the individuals on the team accountable for their commitments and responsibilities. Leaders hold themselves accountable, model appropriate behaviors, and enforce standards. Obvious indicators that leadership was a root cause: the leader was late, didn't communicate expectations, was unreachable during the execution phase, missed the team training, or didn't discipline a team member for an infraction.

Organization

Defining the roles of all the team members and identifying the relevant processes and documents necessary to guide the team is a fundamental requirement of organization. Organization in this sense is about the *physical organization* of things, the *clarity of roles* and responsibilities, and the *coordination of communication* protocols and meetings. A poorly organized meeting without the supporting documents is an all-too-frequent root cause for a sales presentation gone bad.

Communication

Communication refers to sharing, coordinating, and disseminating relevant information. If Andy, for some reason outside his control, couldn't accomplish his assigned task within the COA when he was supposed to, and never told anyone until the mission drew hopelessly past the deadline, that's a failure to communicate. Good communication also includes a clear and complete understanding of individual responsibilities. In assigning responsibilities, the team leader repeats the assignments, makes eye contact with the team member and asks if that was clear. There are only two answers: yes or no.

Communication should also be two-way, so everyone on the team has a good mental picture of what's going on. We call that *situational awareness*. Situational awareness is the quality of an individual or organization's mental model of the real world. Without clear and frequent communication, situational awareness deteriorates, which undermines effectiveness, impairs judgment, reduces relevancy, and increases the likelihood of missed opportunities. The deterioration of good situational awareness can also lead to Task Saturation among individual team members.

Knowledge

The next two characteristics, knowledge and experience, are closely related but not the same. Knowledge is the "know *what*" and experience is the "know *how*." Knowledge deals with the acquisition, identification and utilization of information. It can be written down and passed from one individual to the next. Teams can collaborate to share and even create knowledge. They should also seek the best information available when planning and making decisions.

The absence of knowledge manifests itself in a number of ways. Not having basic data at your fingertips—how many steaks do you sell on a Saturday night, what is the new format for compressed video— would be a failure of knowledge. Not having experienced or used something essential to a plan would be a failure of tacit knowledge or experience, the subject of the next category.

Experience

Experience helps bridge the gap between the known and the unknown. Teams should seek to include individuals with relevant experience whenever possible. Debriefing should also be conducted regularly in order to accelerate experience in each team member. It is difficult to sell something about which you have no direct experience. Experience is similar to tacit knowledge. Have you ever flown an F-15, run a manufacturing plant, or developed a new product?

Discipline

Finally, discipline is about focusing the team on the right things and keeping progress on track. Having discipline means adhering to standards, processes, guiding principles and stated values. It also means carrying out the COA and responding to contingencies as planned. Simply, discipline is doing what you are supposed to do.

Root Causes Category 4: Execution

What interfered with the execution of the plan? After years of root cause analysis, military aviators still find themselves looking at problems for which none of the preceding root causes provided an adequate answer. There was something missing that defied ordinary categorization, and yet this mysterious phenomenon began to take shape and form. In time, the missing root cause was given a name: Task Saturation.

Task Saturation

You simply have too much to do—or at least you *think* you have too much to do. That was the missing root cause; you're Task Saturated. You can't plug the refueling boom, manage the radios, stay in a tight formation on the tanker and watch for enemy aircraft all at the same time, and guess what? You snap the boom because you're Task Saturated.

The most pernicious performance-draining phenomenon is Task Saturation. Task Saturation is the perception or reality that you have too much to do and too little time or resources with which to do it. When Task Saturation sets in, people start using coping mechanisms, most of which lead to other problems. Rather than shedding tasks, they channelize and focus on just one thing to the detriment of other more important things. Rather than using checklists, crosschecks, or mutual support from someone on the team, they shut down or simply throw up their hands and give up.

Here are some effective ways to mitigate Task Saturation that, if missed, are significant root causes for error.

Crosschecks – Priorities

Task Saturation can cause people to lose focus on priorities. In aviation, Task Saturation is mitigated by the layout of the cockpit instrument panel. An instrument panel has one central-most important gauge: the attitude indicator, the gauge that displays the aircraft's orientation to the ground. The other gauges surrounding the attitude indicator provide other information. In order to keep attention on the attitude indicator, pilots learn a hub-and-spoke scan pattern with their eyes in which the attitude indicator is checked first, then a peripheral indicator, then back to the attitude indicator, and then to a different gauge, and so forth. That is the crosscheck pattern. Analogously, individuals and teams manage priorities in a similar way by always keeping their mind and eyes first and foremost on what is, at present, their single most important priority.

Mutual Support

A high-performing team functions as a single entity when team members provide mutual support. They are not afraid to point out when someone is making a mistake, not because they are being critical but because they care about the success of the whole team. Teammates are committed to identifying behaviors that are "dumb, different, or dangerous." Teams with highly refined supportive instincts are especially sensitive to activities that may be dangerous or differ from the briefed plan. High-performing teams possess the courage to address such issues instantly.

Checklists

People smile when I tell them that a fighter pilot's best friend is a checklist. We have checklists for engine start, taxi, takeoff, landing, and all sorts of in-flight emergencies. If my mind shuts down or if I get hopelessly Task Saturated, I have my checklists.

Checklists are a simple tool that can aid execution in big ways. In the past few years, checklists have been recognized for their measurable positive impact on the improvement of quality. Through recent research, the medical profession has demonstrated that checklists even improve team performance and reduce medical errors—and save lives.[1] One study demonstrated a 47% improvement to mortality rates when checklists were used in conjunction with post-operative debriefings.

X-Gap Meetings

An X-Gap Meeting is probably unlike any meeting you've ever attended. It's more like an execution fitness session complete with a personal trainer. They are short, focused, and intense with a dual purpose. X-Gap meetings hold everyone accountable for their individual commitments and make necessary changes to the plan and/or reallocate resources. Much has been proven about the efficacy of commitments and transparent actions within teams. Shining a bright light upon the accountable actions of every member of the team pays big dividends in improved teamwork and execution. The X-Gap meeting does just that, and it does it on a regular basis. An X-Gap Meeting is where the leader of a team brings the team together to review a day, week, or a few weeks of work toward some well-defined objective. The format of the meeting looks quickly at every task, assesses progress, seeks reasons for failure and adjusts the plan or reallocates resources as necessary.

X-gap Meetings are one of the most effective tools to block Task Saturation, as well as many other root causes that creep into teams and hurt performance.

And that's it: four categories with twenty-one root causes. Do these twenty-one things right and you are as close to a guaranteed win as possible in our uncertain world. Get them wrong or ignore them and increase your chances of missing the mark.

When you perform root cause analysis and get down to one or just a few root causes, you address them in a lesson learned. But those root causes need to be noted and cascaded upward in the organization for review at higher levels. When collected throughout an organization, root causes provide the capacity for identification of recurring root causes. That is, an organization can look at those issues that consistently recur and address them on a larger scale.

Just as the Air Force and the Navy recognized the recurring root causes of training and experience and established the debriefing process to address them, any organization can take advantage of this process to excel. That's improvement on a grand scale. To see how this might work, refer to Appendix D for an example of recurring root cause analysis and cascading debriefing at the strategic level in a Fortune 500 company.

Root Cause Identification Matrix

1 - Core	2 - Planning	3 - Team	4 - Execution
PEOPLE Hiring practices and screening; Employment Policy; sufficient external labor resources	**OBJECTIVE** Clear, measurable, achievable and supports strategy and Future Picture	**LEADERSHIP** Leader holds self and team accountable, models appropriate behaviors, and enforces standards; (resist temptation to cite as catch-all)	**TASK SATURATION** Too much to do and too little time to do it; mitigated by the practices below
TRAINING Knowledge and skills that should exist given known or anticipated needs	**THREATS** Risks assessed to include known threats and "known unknown" threats	**ORGANIZATION** Physical organization of things; unambiguous roles and responsibilities; organization and coordination of meetings	**CROSSCHECKS – PRIORITIES** Prioritize and execute to the highest priorities first, particularly when Task Saturated
STANDARDS Defined processes, instructions, guidance, or doctrine	**RESOURCES** Available resources identified to negate, mitigate, or avoid threats – additional needed resources identified	**COMMUNICATION** Brief plans; maintain clear expectations and alignment between individual activity and Future Picture; maintain situational awareness	**MUTUAL SUPPORT** Team members support and value each other; take responsibility to point out 'dumb, different, and dangerous'; aid others that are Task Saturated
STRATEGY Plan is clear, measurable, achievable, and supports the achievement of the Future Picture	**LESSONS LEARNED** Draw upon experience of team / entire organization and lessons learned databases to improve plan	**KNOWLEDGE** Collaborate and include cognitive diversity on the team; seek the best information available	**CHECKLISTS** Use wherever appropriate; utilize course of action as a checklist
FUTURE PICTURE Clear, compelling and high-resolution	**COURSE OF ACTION** Clear, written course of action with "who, what, and when"; Reviewed through Red Teaming	**EXPERIENCE** Include both novices and experts on team; debrief to accelerate experience	**X-GAP** Short, focused team meetings to analyze execution to date and close execution gaps
	CONTINGENCIES Planned response to threats with clear triggers	**DISCIPLINE** Adherence to standards and plans	

Takeaways

- To develop the most effective lessons learned, seek out root causes and address them. Be consistent in the categorization of root causes by utilizing standard categories.
- Standardizing root causes will aid in the analysis of recurring root causes so they may be effectively addressed on a large scale.

A LIFE OF CONTINUOUS
IMPROVEMENT

SO FAR WE'VE DESCRIBED debriefing as an event that concludes another event. We've noted how root causes help us inject lessons learned into the system. But these definitions fall short of bringing this full circle and explaining how debriefing fits into our everyday lives. When my engine flamed out over the Pacific Ocean, my first reactions were a by-product of a spike of adrenaline. You can imagine —single-seat fighter at 30,000 feet, at night in bad weather, and your cockpit turns into a bank of yellow and red flashing lights while an automated voice barks inside my helmet, "Warning FTIT overtemp right engine, warning FTIT overtemp right engine ..." There I was, 26 years old, hundreds of miles from land, dealing with a possible emergency in a 30-million-dollar fighter jet over a storm-tossed ocean.

Thankfully, I had a checklist. The checklist on my kneeboard was the product of millions of hours of flight time and hundreds of engine problems identical to my own. Each of those emergencies had been debriefed and analyzed and from each came a lesson learned, the sum of which was strapped on my leg.

My training kicked in. I flipped to the pages for *Single Engine Stall Stagnation Procedures* and the words I so desperately wanted were right there, in boldface type. Step one. Step Two. Step Three. Not a single unnecessary word. Every step I needed to relight my engine.

Procedures, processes, lessons learned; these things are the fabric of our lives whether they are strapped on to us as a kneeboard or incorporated in our personal standards and personal approaches to life. Consider the "Miracle on the Hudson." Three minutes after takeoff, Captain Chelsey "Sully" Sullenberger's Airbus A320 slammed into a flock of Canadian geese. Both engines ingested birds and lost power.

US Airways Flight 1549 suddenly became a powerless glider with just a few thousand feet of air beneath its wings. Sully considered turning back to LaGuardia, but he was losing altitude so he made the decision to take the nearest "runway" he could find; he ditched in the Hudson River. Although it was a bitterly cold day in January, 2009, all 155 souls on board escaped safely.

Chelsey Sullenberger was a former Air Force fighter pilot. In 1980, he turned in his flight suit and joined the airlines. Twenty-nine years later, his entire career as an aviator was called into action. Every experience he had would be folded into the next three minutes. Well, would you be ready? Think about it. Think about 29 years and countless training sessions with their repetitive checklists for this emergency or that emergency. How many years can you be tested on the same checklist before you want to go crazy? How boring could it get? How much easier would it be to go into yearly check rides resting on past experiences, and be unprepared for the unthinkable or unexpected?

For Sully, slacking off would have been impossible. That's not what pilots do. Training keeps us alive—and in this case, it kept 155 people alive. Sully was cited for exceptional cockpit resource management, praise that means more to an aviator than being elected to the Hall of Fame. Sully was a walking textbook of lessons learned, a man who lived by his lessons learned every time he strapped into a jet. Lessons learned are the things that guide us, help us make good decisions, keep us from making preventable mistakes. That's how debrief fits into our everyday lives. One lesson learned builds upon another until we have a way of life imprinted on our very being.

Flawless is unattainable; but the pursuit of flawless is a way of life characterized by some internal drive to be the best. We pay attention to our training because we know it incorporates the experiences of those before us and we don't want to repeat their mistakes. We demand of ourselves the discipline required to perform at a high level because we know the absence of discipline is a root cause of failures.

We use checklists to save our lives, to prevent a plan from failing. And we celebrate wins, end things with a smile, give others a high note to end their day. All of this flows into those moments that define us and our characters.

As a 25-year old lieutenant, my writing partner on this book was walking up to the bridge to report for duty for his shift as officer of the deck on the aircraft carrier USS *Theodore Roosevelt*. Officer of the Deck carries with it enormous responsibility: making sure the ship is headed where it's supposed to be headed, ensuring flight operations are carried out as scheduled, and taking care of the thousands of other daily activities that are life on an aircraft carrier. Unless the ship's captain says otherwise, the Officer of the Deck is running the show.

But he doesn't just walk up a few decks, salute and start his shift. First he stops at Central Control, the main engineering station for the two nuclear reactors and all the other machinery that supply the energy for this city at sea. The Engineering Officer of the Watch and crew run down the important items, including the status of the power plants, main engines, the power grid and any special plans or tests to be carried out over the next 4 hours, the length of his watch.

Next, he goes to the Combat Information Center to be briefed by the Tactical Action Officer. This is an intense, battle-ready room filled with radar scopes and electronic displays that runs the defensive armaments of the ship. These guys watch everything that's happening in the air, on and under the sea, and even on the land nearby for a thousand miles in every direction. So he gets a full status report on threats in the area, weapons, air defense systems—everything he needs to know about the combat status of the carrier.

Next he goes up to the Tactical Operations Plot to get a visual picture of what ships are where on the surface of the sea. It's not a good thing to turn to the right and ram a tanker you didn't know was there.

Only then, armed with a vivid sense of the aircraft carrier's position, situation and status, does he step on the bridge. But, again, he makes the rounds—navigation, communications, radar, conning officer—and after updates from the officers on the bridge, then and only then is he ready to relieve the current Officer of the Deck.

The captain, leaning back in his massive chair, exhausted from a 36-hour transit through the Suez Canal, looks up as the lieutenant approaches and salutes. "Good evening Captain, I am ready to relieve the Deck," he says. The captain returns his salute and says, "Very well, I'll be in my cabin for the rest of the evening, have a good night." "Captain's off the bridge," announces the Boatswain's Mate of the Watch as the captain disappears down the dark passageway behind the helm console. "I relieve you, sir," he says, saluting. "I stand relieved," says the previous Officer of the Deck, returning his salute.

And with that, as the sun set over the dunes along the shores of Egypt and the captain retired for some badly needed sleep, the USS *Theodore Roosevelt* emerged from the mouth of the Suez Canal into the Gulf of Suez, bound for the open waters of the Red Sea with a 25 year-old lieutenant unexpectedly running the show. With more than 100,000 tons of bombs, bullets, aircraft, fuel, food, reactors, 5,000 sailors, and steel, he had been handed the keys by a captain exhausted by a difficult 36 hours on the bridge.

> "The combination of valid data from a number of external sources, broad communication of that information inside an organization, and a willingness to deal honestly with the feedback will go a long way toward squashing complacency."
>
> –John P. Kotter, Leading Change

He carried it off without a hitch. That's what we mean by acquiring knowledge. The absence of knowledge is a root cause of failure, and he was trained to know that, so he made his rounds before he stepped on the bridge. He was ready to assume the responsibilities of Officer of the Deck of one of the world's most impressive military assets. On arriving, he was thrust into circumstances that were both unusual and beyond his control. Rather than simply reporting for duty, they needed him to step into some big shoes. With night falling and the narrow waters of the Gulf of Suez, with ships all around him and the captain now resting, it was a good time to be task saturated. Maybe he was. But he had armed himself with knowledge before he arrived and, facing an unexpected, awesome responsibility, he did the right thing— he let mutual support kick in. He had good people on the bridge. He let them do their jobs.

Debriefing isn't merely an event that takes place at the end of another event. It's a catalyst for a way of life. The plan-brief-execute-debrief cycle leads to continuous improvement because it continuously generates new lessons learned that flow into our inventory of experiences and knowledge. It's up to us to incorporate those lessons learned into our daily activity. I owe my executional excellence to the thousands of pilots who came before me. I owe my checklists to the pilots who came before me. These are the very things that guide us, help us make good decisions, keep us from making preventable mistakes.

Remember, it isn't who's right; it's what's right!

Takeaway

- Debriefing is commitment to lifelong learning and a tool of continuous improvement.

Appendix A: STEALTH DEBRIEF CHECKLIST

STEALTH DEBRIEF CHECKLIST
Debrief:

- At the end of a project, plan or mission

- In response to an unexpected event

- Frequently, when plans or projects exceed the span of several weeks or a month

S - Set Time – Before you begin your mission, determine the location, start time, and end time of the debrief.
T - **Tone** – "Nameless and Rankless" debrief. Leader opens by admitting own mistakes.
E - **Execution versus Objectives** – Repeat the mission objective and compare actual execution to that objective. List the successes and errors.

Identifying Results Framework
1. Did we execute as planned?
2. Were the individual tasks within the plan *effective*?
3. Overall, what went wrong?

A - Analyze Execution – Determine the direct causes of the successes and errors in the execution, "*How* did it happen?" Then dive deeper to determine their root causes.

Root Causes Matrix			
Core	Planning	Team	Execution
People	Objective	Leadership	Task Saturation
Training	Threats	Organization	Crosschecks
Standards	Resources	Communication	Mutual Support
Strategy	Lessons Learned	Knowledge	Checklists
Vision	Course of Action	Experience	X-Gap
	Contingencies	Discipline	

L - Lessons Learned – Develop step-by-step actions that address the root causes in order to improve future execution. Keep the lesson learned in context by including the following components:

1. **Results** – The results may be positive or negative, a success or error. Define the result in simple terms and do not relate it to causes.

2. **Cause** – The cause is typically the obvious or the apparent cause of the failure or success. It may not be the underlying or root cause, but it certainly led to the result.

3. **Root Cause** – This is the underlying cause that will correspond to one of the categories from the Root Cause Identification Matrix.

4. **Lesson Learned** – Lessons learned should be specific such that specific actions are clearly written down to guide future teams to repeat a success or prevent an error.

5. **Single Point of Accountability** (SPA) – Appoint an individual who will be held accountable for taking action on the lesson learned and transferring it.

6. **Timeline** – This is the date when the SPA will have accomplished the task assigned to implement the results of the lessons learned.

T - Transfer Lessons Learned – Communicate lessons learned to the team and store them for easy reference.

H - High Note – Positively summarize the accomplishments of the plan or project.

Debrief Record		
Mission Objective:		
Result(s):		
Cause(s):		
Root Cause(s):		
Lesson Learned:	1.	
	2.	
	3.	
	4.	
	5.	
	6.	
SPA:		
Timeline:		

Appendix B: STEALTH DEBRIEFING CASE 1

Knowledge Partners was off to a good start. They had a client, they had a product to sell, they were on the road, and they just needed four more clients to quit their day jobs and jump in full time. So they scheduled three meetings with three national vendors to make sales presentations. They hoped their presentations would demonstrate how their services could improve a potential client's data and decision-making, and positively impact their bottom line.

The first meeting went poorly. A third partner was responsible for the actual data mining process. It was their job to query the more than 125 million rows of data and turn it into impressive charts and graphs. Unfortunately, a software upgrade unexpectedly caused errors in the final product during a demonstration before the first potential client. The result was an embarrassing display of fumbling and perceived incompetence—and a lost sale.

The second meeting yielded an equally poor result. The new software responded painfully slowly. After struggling through five charts, there wasn't much to discuss with the client, just a lot of uncomfortable silence.

Unfortunately, by the third meeting the partners were still making major errors in their presentation. By then they had the data engine running perfectly, and they knew the presentation, so they decided to transfer the software from a server to a laptop that would make a more professional presentation—which was a huge mistake. The data didn't transfer correctly and the laptop did not have enough memory. Worse, the IT partner kept the problem to themselves. Three hours before the meeting, the data was still not working on the laptop. The third meeting resulted in another embarrassment in front of a potential client.

Bob, the only partner who had been exposed to the Stealth Debrief process, had been unable to convince the other partners to take the time to debrief or utilize any of the four components of the Flawless Execution Cycle. After the third failure, "I'd been trying to get our group to do a Stealth Debrief from the very beginning," explained Bob, "but the COO was always in a hurry to get back to his real job, and the IT partner wasn't the type to open up and admit mistakes. But this last meeting was a complete meltdown. We had everything going for us, yet we were our own worst enemy. Instead of landing three new clients, we left three important meetings with egg on our faces. We had to get to the root causes and solve our problem."

Bob locked the doors and forced the partners to do a debrief; it was not a full Stealth Debrief, but it was a start. "We had to do something. I wouldn't let anyone leave the client's conference room until we talked. For some reason my mind focused on the 'nameless, rankless' rule, so that's how I started, by evaluating my own performance, which wasn't so hot. Interestingly, that started the ball rolling. Data mining projects are a lot more difficult than you would believe. Even the smallest change in your processes—a new laptop, a new chart—can affect how the data displays. We began to see how fickle, how sensitive, data can be. So we came up with some lessons learned and made them part of our corporate standards. First, we would not commit to a meeting date until we saw a full dress rehearsal. Second, once we approved the demonstration, we locked down everything and nothing touched that laptop. No new data. No changes in the presentation. Nothing. That's pretty rigid—and it cost us time, but our next meeting went off without a hitch."

Knowledge Partners' first debrief was not a formal Stealth Debrief. But once the value of debriefing had been demonstrated to the partners, they were sold on just how powerful an improvement tool it is. From then on, their debriefs adhered to the Stealth Debrief model.

One can easily see how *Knowledge Partners* utilized the first four steps in the Stealth Debrief process in this case. Although no specific time was set aside for the partners' debrief, it was performed in a timely manner while the execution was fresh in each of their minds; that was the "S." Bob successfully set the ever-critical "T" by admitting his own mistakes first, thus opening up the other partners to frankly admitting theirs.

For the "E" there is a problem. The partners had no explicitly stated objective for each of the three client presentations. Perhaps there was an unspoken and obvious objective as simple as *"On such-and-such a date, time, and place, demonstrate the capabilities of Knowledge Partners to client A and secure a contract for services in the sum of X dollars."* But that was not spelled out as such, and therefore could not be measured. Therefore, one may only assume that the objective was not achieved. Such a lack of a clear, measurable, and achievable objective is a candidate for a root cause; it is one of the six root causes under the planning category.

Furthermore, for the "A," analyze execution, there is also an obvious potential root cause. The partners apparently had no written course of action that expressly detailed the tasks that each partner would be responsible to perform in support of the unclear and unstated objective. Again, there is a potential error under the planning category. So before the partners begin to dig into the causes and root causes of the execution, they have already discovered two potential root causes: unclear or missing objective and course of action.

Still, *Knowledge Partners* have more to debrief. They know that they had three opportunities, all meeting with failure. They can ask themselves what, specifically, were those failures. In each case, the failure can simply be stated as a failure to make a sale; but in each case, the cause is different. In the first presentation the cause was unexpected errors in the software. In the second, the cause was slow responsiveness of the software. The third presentation failed because of an inadequate laptop. Those three things were the results they would take and focus upon in a root cause analysis.

They ask why each cause occurred without naming names or blaming the failures on things outside the organization's control. They determine the root cause from one of those twenty-one items. For the first failure, the partners list several items: standards and experience. For the second failure, they list those same things and add to them the lack of checklists for conducting sales presentations. Analysis of the third failure would uncover the same root causes.

Knowledge Partners Debriefs		
Presentation 1	**Presentation 2**	**Presentation 3**
Failure: Lost Sale	Failure: Lost Sale	Failure: Lost Sale
Cause: Software Errors	Cause: Software Speed	Cause: Inadequate Laptop
Root Cause(s): Standards Experience	Root Cause(s): Standards Experience Checklists	Root Cause(s): Standards Checklists

In the *Knowledge Partners* case study, the partners recognized that they lacked a standard operating procedure for sales presentations in all three cases. Their lesson learned should address that need in a series of actionable steps. The lesson learned is not that the standard operating procedure needs to be developed; instead, the lesson learned should *outline a plan or course of action* that the partners will take after the debrief to address the root cause. For example, the actionable lesson learned from the case study might look like this:

1. Develop a sales presentation Standard Operating Procedure (SOP).
2. Elements to include in this SOP: testing the equipment and software, rehearsing the presentation.
3. Meet at 10:00 on Tuesday to develop a SOP.
4. Bob will lead this effort.

The debrief is not the place to engage major projects. In the *Knowledge Partners* case, they realized that they had to address a major root cause issue that would require a considerable investment in time. Of course, in the regular practice of debriefing this will not always be the case. Most debriefs will result in simple, actionable lessons learned.

Knowledge Partners is a new organization that is obviously inexperienced with sales and is perhaps in need of some additional technical knowledge. But knowledge and experience can be addressed through proper standards. As indicated in chapter 1, standards provide guidance toward a minimum level of execution; they are the basics for getting the job done the right way. The partners came to recognize just how much the possession of good standards, and a disciplined adherence to them, could mean to the future of their business. It is also from standards that organizations can create excellent checklists to support proper execution.

An organization's first experience with Stealth Debriefing is typically similar to that of *Knowledge Partners*. The root cause analysis reveals significant issues to address. It also underscores why a complete Flawless Execution Cycle of plan-brief-execute-debrief is a far more powerful tool than debriefing alone.

Appendix C: STEALTH DEBRIEFING CASE 2

Knowledge Partners had a rocky start, but the company is now standing firmly on its own two feet and the three partners have happily left their day jobs to run their own business full time. With a strong base of clients, the three partners have won an opportunity to make a sales presentation to their biggest opportunity yet. They sit down and carefully plan their presentation. Their plan looks like this:

Mission Objective: Secure a verbal agreement with Megacorp to provide data management software services on February 2, 2011.		
What	Who	When
1. Research Megacorp / situational profiling	Pradeep	Jan 24
2. Meet with Kim to develop client needs questions	Pradeep	Jan 25
3. Update the presentation slides with appropriate client info	Pradeep	Jan 26
4. Upload the data and slide presentation to the presentation laptop in accordance with the standards	Kim	Jan 27
5. Develop a customized value proposition for Megacorp	Bob	Jan 27
6. Rehearse the presentation	Bob et al	Jan 28
7. Red Team the presentation with YPO peers.	Bob et al	Jan 29
8. Deliver presentation	Bob	Feb 2
9. Drive presentation and demonstrate software capabilities	Kim	Feb 2
10. Observe, take notes, and provide contextual understanding	Pradeep	Feb 2
11. Ask for the business	Bob	Feb 2
12. If no, develop contingency next steps	Bob	Feb 2
13. Confirm follow-on meeting	Bob	Feb 2
14. Thank and review with client	Bob	Feb 2
15. Debrief	Bob	Feb 2

By the morning of February 2, the big day, the partners were feeling pretty good. They had accomplished everything so far in the course of action. They were even lucky enough to get a few of their friends from the local Young Presidents Organization to act as a Red Team and sit through their presentation and offer valuable pointers for improvement. They were ready for the big opportunity at Megacorp.

According to their plan, Bob was in charge of sales and marketing and would run the presentation. Kim, the technical whiz, would drive the slide presentation and the demonstration of the software. Pradeep, the head of operations for *Knowledge Partners*, would take notes and back up Bob and Kim if needed. They arrived at Megacorp on schedule and their meeting with the CIO began right on time. Unfortunately, they fell short of the mission objective; they did not secure the verbal agreement they had hoped for. On their way back to the office, they talked about what could have gone wrong, but stopped short of making conclusions until they could perform a complete debrief.

Upon their return to the office, they all took a quick break and agreed to meet in the conference room precisely at 3 pm.

Bob: "This was my presentation and we didn't get the sale. So ultimately I own this loss. I'm not sure exactly why we lost the sale because, from my perspective, I thought we all did a great job. But I know I forgot a very important thing; I didn't ask for the business. I know this was what we planned, but I think that by the end of the presentation I got a bit flustered. I could tell from the CIO's questions and the expression on his face that I had not won him over. I have to be more mindful of that in the future."

Kim: "Yeah, Bob, no question about it. We didn't get the sale. But you did a great job. Let's see if we can figure out why we lost this one. Pradeep, do you agree? Did we execute as we planned this?"

Pradeep: "Sure we did. With the exception of Bob's mistake, we did what we said we would do. And I agree with Bob, we lost that sale before he forgot to ask for the business. His was just a minor error."

Bob: "Thanks Pradeep, I won't let that happen again. Now, let's take a look at our course of action in detail. What about task #1? Did you research this thing carefully?"

Pradeep: "I think I did. Although the CIO was pretty stone-faced and silent throughout most of the presentation, I saw several affirmative nods during the introduction."

Kim: "True, I saw them too. But that doesn't mean we had the right info. Even if Bob did the best research possible, you don't know what you don't know!"

Bob: "Okay then, what about the client needs questions?"

Kim: "I thought that went great. The CIO was very forthcoming and we asked all the right technical questions."

Pradeep: "I agree. From the responses I observed, we really engaged the CIO and showed that we knew our stuff."

Bob: "All right, moving on, I think we all agree that the technical aspects of our presentation were flawless. Thanks Kim. But what about task #5, the value proposition?"

Pradeep: "I gotta say, Bob, I think that's where things began to unravel. It just didn't seem to resonate with the CIO."

Kim: "Yep, there's definitely something we're missing there."

Bob: "Okay, I'll make a note of that as one of our results and we'll review that later. Now, what about the rehearsal?"

Kim: "That went great, and so did the Red Team with our YPO buddies."

Pradeep: "Thumbs up on those two."

Bob: "Alright then, tasks eight, nine, and ten concerned our individual roles in the presentation. We already agreed that Kim did a great job and that I could have done better. Pradeep, what about you? As backup, was there anything you observed?"

Pradeep: "There was no one thing, Bob; the CIO just seemed to become more and more disinterested as the presentation progressed."

Bob: "We already know that I blew it on task #11. So what about task #12?"

Kim: "Well, we all saw what happened. We couldn't counter his objections. We weren't prepared for some tough questions."

Bob: "Kim, you're right. But why weren't we prepared? Let's take a look at those objections. What was the biggest one?"

Pradeep: "That our application is web-based? Though he didn't come right out and say it, he kept emphasizing that point in his questioning."

Bob: "No, I don't think that's exactly it. Why would a web-based application be objectionable to a CIO?"

Kim: "Oh, right, I think I'm following you now, Bob. It's not that our application is web-based, it's that a CIO is concerned with security and because the software is actually running on our servers rather than the client's, that might be perceived as a threat to their information security."

Pradeep: "Okay, but our program can run on their servers too. It doesn't have to reside on ours. That would give them a better sense of security, rather than relying on ours."

Bob: "Bottom line is that we didn't volunteer that information to alleviate the fear in the first place. We should have done a better job and anticipated that sort of objection. So that's another result. Now, for the next two tasks, I didn't ask for a follow-on because I was so flustered from the CIO's cold response to our presentation. And, although I was thankful, I didn't review the meeting. Had I reviewed, it might have given us an opportunity to address some of the fears we outlined."

The team had now progressed through every step in their plan. On a white board in the conference room, Bob had summarized the results so far. It looked like this:

TASK	EFFECTIVE?
1. Research Megacorp / situational profiling	Unclear
2. Meet with Kim to develop client needs questions	Yes
3. Update the presentation slides with appropriate client info	Yes
4. Upload the data and slide presentation to the presentation laptop in accordance with the standards	Yes
5. Develop a customized value proposition for Megacorp	Unclear
6. Rehearse the presentation	Yes
7. Red Team the presentation with YPO peers.	Yes
8. Deliver presentation	Yes
9. Drive presentation and demonstrate software capabilities	Yes
10. Observe, take notes, and provide contextual understanding	Unclear
11. Ask for the business	No
12. If no, develop contingency next steps	No
13. Confirm follow-on meeting	No
14. Thank and review with client	No
15. Debrief	Yes

With the details of the plan's execution analyzed, the team took a step back and asked what, after all those errors, led to the ultimate failure of their mission. They pondered for a few minutes. Suddenly Bob slapped his hand against his forehead and sighed.

Bob: "Guys, I think we have the wrong mission objective."

Pradeep: "What do you mean?"

Bob: "Who is the client?"

Kim: "Megacorp?"

Bob: "No, it's not. It's Megacorp's *CIO*. We planned to an objective that was wrong. Just think how differently we would have planned if we had really realized who it was we were pitching to. We pitched like we were talking to the CEO and operational executives. We have a product that is valuable to executives like that. But for a CIO, our application is just another headache to manage."

Pradeep: "You're right, Bob! I got this sales call set up through Megacorp's COO, who I met last month at the technology expo. She was so excited about our product then. Now that I think back, she specifically said that she wanted to run it through the CIO. That's how I got us set up for the sales call. I should have realized that she meant this was a technical review of our product."

Kim: "And who were all the folks that helped us out by acting as a Red Team?"

Pradeep: "Oh man, those guys all run operations-oriented businesses, just the kind of people who would love our application. There wasn't a single individual with an IT background on the Red Team. We completely missed the boat on this one."

With this three-step approach, Knowledge Partners identified some very specific results. By merely asking if they executed as planned, they did not have enough critical analysis to accurately answer that question. It was only by analyzing the *effectiveness* of each task and then stepping back to look at those results as a whole that they were able to identify the results of their mission and assemble a possible underlying cause for their mission's failure.

Appendix D: DEBRIEFING AT EVERY LEVEL: STEALTH DEBRIEFING CASE 3

In military terms, the word "tactical" refers to frontline operations. It is the means by which the soldier or the military unit achieves victory on the battlefield. To be *tactical* means to be concerned with the details of executing short-range objectives. To be *strategic*, on the other hand, means to be concerned with higher-order, long-range objectives. All organizations have both tactical and strategic activities. Tactical activities are those that concern day-to-day operational planning and execution.

Tactical Debriefing

In Stealth Debriefing Cases #1 and #2, a new company composed of only a few individuals debriefed tactically for the first time and uncovered numerous root causes, which is typical of a new, small company. This chapter presents a tactical debriefing case study within a large, mature Fortune 500 company with well-established planning procedures and comprehensive written standards.

The concepts and practices presented in the preceding chapters are demonstrated in this real-world case study. Specifically, the debrief will cover a typical monthly planning rhythm in which production is planned to achieve monthly goals. Tactical debriefing should occur frequently to align with short-term objectives, make adjustments and improvements, develop lessons learned, and provide root cause analysis. Frequent root cause analysis provides the basic data that can be reviewed at higher organizational levels and over longer timeframes in order to identify and target underlying organizational issues.

Stealth Debriefing Case 3

In support of a national campaign plan with a desired effect of improving productivity, a single district within a large national corporation has planned a monthly mission. This service company relies upon a large number of service personnel and a supporting fleet of service vehicles (vans). The mission objective is to improve productivity by 2% for the upcoming month.

Mission Objective: Improve previous-year-same-month productivity by 2% (6.78) for month ending July 31, 2010.

The district executes its plan and, as the last task in the course of action for that plan, the management team sits down at a predetermined place and time to perform a Stealth Debrief.

The general manager, leader of the team, opens the debrief promptly at 9:00 am in the designated conference room. All staff who planned the mission are present and seated on time. At each seat, the GM has placed the preceding month's productivity reports and some other supporting material. The productivity report clearly shows that the district fell short of its mission objective by 0.3%.

He begins by asking everyone what their mission objective was. They respond quickly and properly. He is forthcoming from the start and admits that, "Although I believe you all executed the mission well, the objective I presented may have been too ambitious. To improve productivity as greatly as 2% in a single month was challenging. I took a look at the annual goals and ran the numbers again. The actual results for this month's productivity have us on track to meet our year-end goals. I may have pushed a little too hard this month, but this team put forth a great effort. So let's take a look at what happened, learn from it, and build a lead on productivity goals going into the last half of this year."

The team jumps in and analyzes each task in the course of action. Each manager shows similar shortfalls towards their objectives. However, a trend appears as each manager reviews their individual results; the majority of the individual service technicians' productivity scores surpass the objective. It is a few, very low scores in each manager's workgroups that hurt the district's overall score.

As they continue to analyze the cause of the low scores, they recognize a trend. Each manager reports unusually high numbers of breakdowns in their fleet of vans. "It's been a hot summer, and with the added strain of service personnel putting in longer hours, the older vans are failing to keep up." The team quickly calculates the number of van failures. Calculations indicate that van failures increased 10% over the preceding month, and in comparison to annual statistics show the failure rate 7% greater than the same month last year. "Well, that seems to be a significant impact to productivity, with our highly paid service staff sitting idly on the side of the road while waiting for a tow and a replacement van!"

The team begins discussing the root causes of the extremely high rates of van failures. They discover that most of the vans that failed over the past month were some of the oldest in the fleet, with more than 250,000 miles on their odometers. "So," pipes up one manager, "are we saying that our aging fleet is the cause of our productivity shortfall? It's normal to run these vans past 300,000 miles before replacing them." One of the managers speaks out, "Well, I have to admit that almost all the failures in my workgroup were with service personnel that I know don't keep up with their regular maintenance program. I've been meaning to track that more closely and monitor their adherence to the program, but with the pressure to get productivity up, I just put it on the back burner for a while." The other managers concur that failed van maintenance is a clear trend in each of their workgroups.

"So," interjects the district manager "what are the root causes we see here?" The managers lower their heads in thought.

"The standards?"

"Really? What's wrong with the standards?"

"Nothing is wrong with the standards. We and every district in the country use these standards and they don't have van failures at such a high rate."

"I think we've already noticed the root cause. We failed as leaders. We all should have taken a closer look at the maintenance program and held our technicians accountable for it."

"Yeah, you're right, and I know this is going to sound like making excuses, but weren't we a little Task Saturated with such a high productivity goal, and keeping up with the pace in one of the busiest months of the year?"

"All true," interjects the district manager. "We didn't fail to execute to our priorities. We just lost sight of some peripheral—but very important—responsibilities. We lacked discipline. We have a standard process that we clearly failed to adhere to. Now we have to get back on track."

This robust discussion gets down to the root causes of the district's shortfall, and several are noted. Specifically, the team identifies leadership, Task Saturation, and discipline as root cause errors. The remaining debrief challenge is to determine the lesson learned. How will this team prevent these root cause failures in the future?

During the discussion over lessons learned, the team agrees that, as leaders, they are going to have to coach their service staff on the importance of following a proper van maintenance schedule. And they are also going to have to do a better job monitoring the performance of maintenance. They decide that a centralized maintenance record would be better managed than the five separate ones they now have, and that the team could share, through a rotating schedule, the responsibility of auditing the records and holding the service personnel accountable. They believe that weekly audits will take no more than thirty to sixty minutes. Additionally, they realize that if they rotate the schedule each week from one manager to another, no single person will have to take on the added process responsibility more than once every six to eight weeks.

The district's operations manager volunteers to act as the specific point of accountability (SPA) to ensure that the lesson learned is taken for action by the end of the next day. As the SPA, the operations manager also records the data from the debrief in a simple electronic document.

Debrief Record	
Mission Objective:	Improve previous-year-same-month productivity by 2% (6.78) for month-ending July 31, 2011.
Result(s):	Productivity fell short of the objective by .03%
Cause(s):	High rate of service truck mechanical failures
Root Cause(s):	Leadership, Task Saturation, and Discipline
Lesson Learned:	1. All managers coach their teams on the importance of following the established maintenance program. 2. Create and deploy a centralized maintenance audit file. 3. Draft a rotating auditor schedule for the next two months. 4. Develop a spreadsheet to record all district truck mechanical failures.
SPA:	District Operations Manager
Timeline:	August 4, 2011

"I thank you all for your hard work," says the general manager. "After all, we did achieve a significant improvement in productivity and we are on track to achieve our annual goal. Everyone is to be commended for that. I look forward to planning the next month's objective with you all this afternoon. Great job!"

Strategic Debriefing

With a strong performance recorded for the month, an actionable lessons learned that should pay dividends over the next few months, and a list of root cause errors, the district's general manager has some great information to share at the regional debrief that takes place quarterly. There, the GM will be able to compare regional productivity results to objectives with the regional manager, fellow general managers, and the regional staff team. Perhaps other districts had similar experiences and lessons learned. Perhaps other districts could benefit from the truck audit program.

The regional debriefing will be a strategic one. Each of this company's six regions was tasked with productivity improvement as a component of a national productivity improvement initiative, which was part of a long-range strategic plan spanning several years. The individual district plan debriefed in case study #3 was just one small part of this strategy.

These regional strategic debriefs will follow the same Stealth Debrief process. The strategic plan's objective will also need to be clear, measurable, achievable and support the Future Picture. The difference will be the rich data on root causes. The root causes identified by a half-dozen districts over the course of three months will enable these more senior managers to perform a recurring root cause analysis on a much larger scale. Did other districts, month after month, suffer the same issues with leadership, Task Saturation and discipline? If so, what lessons can be learned from that and how should it be addressed? The standardized categories of root causes permit a rapid and effective analysis of perhaps hundreds of cited root causes.

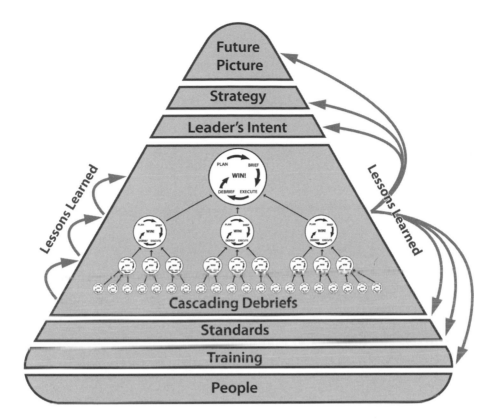

Conclusion

Tactical debriefing can take place on various scales. This case study covered a mission objective and plan that required a month to complete. Tactical debriefing need not cover such a long period or large objective; a simple plan that covers only a day or a few hours is an excellent opportunity, as long as a clear objective has been stated.

Strategic debriefing only differs from tactical debriefing in scale, timeframe and the potential richness of root cause data. The more frequently debriefing is conducted and the more widely it is utilized, the more rapidly and effectively it will transform the organization into a culture of learning.

GLOSSARY

Complex A quality arising from the collective interaction of simple, complicated, or even other complex things distinguished by its unpredictability and incapacity to be fully comprehended.

Contingency Plan A plan or series of plans to respond to anticipated threats when pre-defined indications or triggers that the threat is imminent have occurred.

Continuous Improvement Refers to the improvement of processes.

Course of Action (COA) The core component of a plan that includes the tasks necessary to accomplish the objective. Each task in a proper COA should be assigned to a specific individual with a specific date and/or time by which the task should be accomplished.

Crosschecks An aviation practice in which instruments are monitored in a prioritized hub-and-spoke manner in which the instrument indicating the highest priority information is placed at the center of the instrument panel so its significance is most apparent.

Debriefing A team-centered process of analyzing the results of a plan, project, or mission in order to develop lessons learned and improve future execution.

Flawless Execution A holistic, system of simple, interdependent processes that enables individuals, teams and organizations to accelerate their performance in the rapidly changing, challenging and complex world.

Flawless Execution Cycle The primary, interdependent set of four core processes within the Flawless Execution Model consisting of Plan, Brief, Execute and Debrief.

Flawless Execution Model The complete set of principles and processes that compose Flawless Execution set in a 6-tiered pyramid of Future Picture, Strategy, Leader's Intent, the Flawless Execution Cycle, Standards, Training, and People.

Explicit Knowledge Knowledge that can be written down or otherwise codified for storage and transmission.

Future Picture A clear, compelling, and high-resolution description of the future an organization desires to realize.

High Reliability Organization (HRO) Organizations that operate in high-risk environments with few errors or accidents.

Learning Gap The gap between what an individual, team or organization believes is true about the real world and what is actually true; the misperception of reality.

Lesson Learned A step-by-step set of actions to be taken to address a root cause error; The explicit knowledge product of a debrief.

L.O.C.K.E.D on Teams An acronym indicating the six fundamentals of high-performing teams - leadership, organization, communication, knowledge, experience, and discipline.

Mutual Support Teamwork evidenced by cooperation among individual team members to aid each other to manage Task Saturation, offer constructive criticism, and identify potential sources of error.

Organization (1) a blanket designation for any business, company, government entity, or other association of individuals for some coordinated purpose etc.; (2) the degree to which individuals or members of a team coordinate their activities well.

People What every organization is composed of; the agents of execution.

Process a set of specific steps that converts a specific input into a specific, desired output.

Root Cause Analysis The process within a Stealth Debrief of identifying underlying causes of both errors and successes and assigning them to one of twenty-one general categories.

Standards – the basic guidance, or doctrine, within an organization that guides execution.

Stealth Debriefing A proprietary form of debriefing developed by Afterburner Inc. that follows a disciplined seven-step process corresponding to the acronym S.T.E.A.L.T.H. for Set the Time, Tone, Execution versus Objectives, Analyze Execution, Lesson Learned, Transfer Lesson Learned, and High Note.

Strategic Debriefing The practice of debriefing the progress of longer-range strategic plans and focusing upon addressing recurring root causes of successes and errors.

Strategy – A plan to achieve an organization's Future Picture.

Tacit Knowledge Knowledge that is either impossible or too difficult to codify in written terms. Knowledge that only resides in the human mind - related to the notion of experience.

Tactical Debriefing The practice of debriefing short-range objectives typically performed at the mid to lower operational levels of an organization.

Task Saturation The reality or perception that one has too much to do and too little time or resources to do it.

Training In Flawless Execution, training must align with the Future Picture. Effective training should first be demonstrated then practiced in order to be retained.

ABOUT THE AUTHORS

James D. Murphy

James D. "Murph" Murphy is the founder & CEO of Afterburner, Inc. and author of *Business is Combat,Flawless Execution,* and *The Flawless Execution Field Manual.* He has a unique and powerful mix of leadership skills in both the military and business worlds, including serving in the U.S. Air Force as an F-15 fighter pilot.

Prior to his service in the Air Force, Murph had a successful career in imaging equipment sales, where he helped increase his company's sales by 500%. Years later, he became Director of Sales for a paint company. The concepts he developed and utilized in these businesses and in the Air Force would become known as Flawless Execution™.

Through his leadership, Afterburner Inc. landed on Inc. Magazine's "Inc. 500 List" twice. Murph has been featured in the *Wall Street Journal, BusinessWeek, Inc. Magazine, Newsweek* and *Meetings & Conventions Magazine,* and has appeared on CNN, Fox News, CNBC, ABC, and Bloomberg News. He was named as one of Atlanta's top 50 entrepreneurs by *Catalyst Magazine.* To date, the Afterburner team of elite military professionals has led more than 1 million executives, sales professionals, and business people from every industry through Afterburner's Flawless Execution Model™.

William M. Duke

Will Duke is Afterburner Inc.'s Director of Learning and Development and coauthor of the *Flawless Execution Field Manual* with James D. Murphy. Will has more than 20 years of service as an officer in the U.S. Navy, active and reserve, as well as management experience in both Fortune 500 and small businesses.

He is an expert in organization development and process implementation, including Total Quality Management (TQM), Statistical Process Control, Just-in-Time (JIT), Six Sigma, and ISO 9001. Will currently serves as a senior Human Resources Officer in the U.S. Navy Reserve and has held several command and senior leadership positions.

Other Books by the Authors

Business is Combat: A Fighter Pilot's Guide to Winning in Modern Business Warfare by James D. Murphy (Regan Books / HarperCollins, 2000)

Flawless Execution by James D. Murphy (HarperCollins, 2005)

The Flawless Execution Field Manual by James D. Murphy and William M. Duke (Afterburner Press, 2010)

QUOTATIONS

Page 4: Edgar H. Schein, *Organizational Culture and Leadership*, 3rd Ed. (San Francisco: Jossey-Bass, 2004): 396.

Page 7: Jimmy Guterman, "The Lost Art of Debriefing," *Harvard Business Review* (Vol. 7, No. 3, March 2002).

Page 22: Donald Sull, *The Upside of Turbulence* (New York: Harper Collins, 2009): 167.

Page 29: Noel M. Tichy and Warren G. Bennis, *Judgment: How Winning Leaders Make Great Calls* (Penguin Books, 2007): 84.

Page 31: Karl E. Weick and Kathleen M. Sutcliffe, *Managing The Unexpected: Resilient Performance in an Age of Uncertainty*, 2nd Ed. (San Francisco: John Wiley and Sons, 2007): 33.

Page 39: Jim Collins, *Good To Great: Why Some Companies Make the Leap ... And Others Don't* (HarperCollins, 2001): 78.

Page 45: Ronald Heifetz, Alexander Grashow, and Marty Linsky, *The Practice of Adaptive Leadership* (Boston, Harvard Business Press, 2009): 172.

Page 61: Peter M. Senge, *The Fifth Discipline: The Art and Practice of the Learning Organization* (New York: Doubleday, 2006): 226.

Page 73: John P. Kotter, *Leading Change* (Boston: Harvard Business Press, 1996): 163.

NOTES

Chapter 2

[1] John A. Warden III and Lenand A. Russell, *Winning in FastTime*; (Montgomery, Alabama. Venturist Publishing, 2002) pp 12

[2] John A. Warden III and Lenand A. Russell, *Winning in FastTime*; (Montgomery, Alabama. Venturist Publishing, 2002) pp 16

[3] Noel M. Tichy and Warren G. Bennis, Judgment: How Winning Leaders Make Great Calls (New York: Penguin, 2007) pp 16

[4] John A. Warden III and Lenand A. Russell, *Winning in FastTime*; (Montgomery, Alabama. Venturist Publishing, 2002) pp 17

Chapter 3

[1] Amy C. Edmondson, "The Competitive Imperative of Learning," Harvard Business Review (July-August 2008) 64.

[2] Chris Collison and Jeff Parcell, Learning To Fly: Practical Knowledge Management from Leading and Learning Organizations (West Sussex, England: Capstone Publishing Ltd., 2004) 172.

[3] Michael Hilti, quoted by Heike Bruch and Sumantra Ghoshal in A Bias For Action (Boston: Harvard Business School Press, 2004) 134.

[4] John P. Kotter, Leading Change (Boston: Harvard Business Press, 1996).

[5] Edgar H. Schein, Organizational Culture and Leadership, 3rd Ed. (San Francisco: Jossey-Bass, 2004) 11.

[6] Karl E. Weick and Kathleen M. Sutcliffe, Managing the Unexpected: Resilient Performance in an Age of Uncertainty, 2nd Ed. (San Francisco: Jossey-Bass, 2007) 9.

[7] Ibid: 10.

[8] Ibid: 14.

[9] Jim Collins, <u>How the Mighty Fall: And Why Some Companies Never Give In</u> (New York: HarperCollins, 2009) 78.

Chapter 4
[1] Amy Edmonson, "Psychological Safety and Learning Behavior in Work Teams," <u>Administrative Science Quarterly</u> (June 1999); and Amy Edmonson, "Competitive Imperative of Learning," <u>Harvard Business Review</u> (July-August 2008) 64.

Chapter 6
[1] Atul Gawande, <u>The Checklist Manifesto: How to Get Things Right</u> (Metropolitan Books, 2007); and "An Intervention to Decrease Catheter-Related Bloodstream Infections in the ICU," <u>New England Journal of Medicine</u> (Waltham, MA: December 28, 2006).